IT Services

Costs, Metrics, Benchmarking, and Marketing

ISBN 0-13-019195-7

ENTERPRISE COMPUTING SERIES

▼ Data Warehousing: Architecture and Implementation
Mark Humphries, Michael W. Hawkins, Michelle C. Dy

▼ Software Development: Building Reliable Systems
Marc Hamilton

▼ IT Automation: The Quest for Lights Out
Howie Lyke with Debra Cottone

▼ IT Organization: Building a Worldclass Infrastructure
Harris Kern, Dr. Stuart D. Galup, Guy Nemiro

▼ High Availability: Design, Techniques, and Processes
Michael Hawkins, Floyd Piedad

▼ IT Services: Costs, Metrics, Benchmarking, and Marketing
Anthony F. Tardugno, Thomas R. DiPasquale, Robert E. Matthews

ENTERPRISE COMPUTING SERIES

IT Services

Costs, Metrics, Benchmarking, and Marketing

**Anthony F. Tardugno
Thomas R. DiPasquale
Robert E. Matthews**

PH
PTR
Prentice Hall PTR, Upper Saddle River, NJ 07458
www.phptr.com

Library of Congress Cataloging-in-Publication Data

Tardugno, Anthony F.
   IT services : costs, metrics, benchmarking, and marketing / Anthony F. Tardugno
   Thomas R. DiPasquale, Robert E. Matthews.
      p. cm.
   Includes bibliographical references and index.
   ISBN 0-13-019195-7
      1. Computer service industry. 2. Computer industry–Customer services. I. DiPasquale,
Thomas R. II. Matthews, Robert E. III. Title.

HD9696.67.A2 T37 2000
004.068'8--dc21   00-020112

Editorial/Production Supervision: *Nick Radhuber*
Interior Compositor: *Vanessa Moore*
Acquisitions Editor: *Greg Doench*
Editorial Assistant: *Mary Treacy*
Marketing Manager: *Bryan Gambrel*
Manufacturing Manager: *Alexis Heydt*
Cover Design Direction: *Jerry Votta*
Cover Design: *Anthony Gemmellaro*
Series Design: *Gail Cocker-Bogusz*

© 2000 Prentice Hall PTR
Prentice-Hall, Inc.
Upper Saddle River, NJ 07458

Prentice Hall books are widely used by corporations and government agencies for training, marketing, and resale.

The publisher offers discounts on this book when ordered in bulk quantities.
For more information, contact:
Corporate Sales Department
Prentice Hall PTR
One Lake Street
Upper Saddle River, NJ 07458
Phone: 800-382-3419; fax: 201-236-7141; e-mail: corpsales@prenhall.com

All products or services mentioned in this book are the trademarks or
service marks of their respective owners.

Printed in the United States of America

10 9 8 7 6 5 4 3 2 1

ISBN 0-13-019195-7

Prentice-Hall International (UK) Limited, *London*
Prentice-Hall of Australia Pty. Limited, *Sydney*
Prentice-Hall Canada Inc., *Toronto*
Prentice-Hall Hispanoamericana, S.A., *Mexico*
Prentice-Hall of India Private Limited, *New Delhi*
Prentice-Hall of Japan, Inc., *Tokyo*
Pearson Education Asia Pte. Ltd.
Editora Prentice-Hall do Brasil, Ltda., *Rio de Janeiro*

Dedication

We dedicate this book, our first, to our friends and families for their undying support and encouragement during our pursuit. Thank you for putting up with the long nights, the stress, and the constant requests for proofreading.

Contents

Chapter 2

Getting Started   11

Chapter 3

Establishing and Managing Coalitions—Gaining Buy-In 21

Chapter 4

Business Linkage   29

Chapter 5

Marketing and Communications   41

Chapter 6

Taking a Customer Approach   61

Chapter 11

Measuring Success   131

Appendix B

Sample Service Level Agreement

Index

List of Figures

List of Tables

Preface

It was not our initial intention to write a book dealing with IT services. We were assembled as a team to solve a real business problem. We were given our mission, put on our armor, jumped on our horses, and rode off to *"slay dragons"* in the name of customer satisfaction. The reason we draw this distinction is to point out the advantage this has for you, the reader, of being able to see demonstrated and proven results. It becomes obvious as you progress through each chapter that you are not getting a bunch of theory or unproved strategy. Instead, you are getting the benefit of a strategy and approach that has been implemented and refined, and is providing results.

It is without question that we now live in an age where customer satisfaction is the primary motivating factor among industries. Businesses are focusing their efforts toward improved, expeditious, and more convenient products and services. There is a growing customer "obsession" that is having a net effect not only on what products and services a company or organization is offering, but how they are organized to deliver them. IT services are no exception.

In the not too distant past, business was tied to its internal IT shop as the "only game in town" to deliver their requirements. With consulting and outsourcing strongly making their way onto the scene in the early nineties, the need to get services "inside" has waned, opening up delivery options to the business. This competition alone has probably done more for customer satisfaction than any single factor in the IT arena.

As a business manager and customer of IT services, you want the most cost-effective solution that best meets your requirements regardless of who delivers them. As an IT provider of services, you want to maximize customer satisfaction by optimizing the level of service and optimizing cost. Whether the service delivery remains in-house or goes outside is almost immaterial. The delivery must go to the supplier most capable of delivering to the metrics defined. It is meeting or exceeding the customer's requirements that matters most.

The "knowledge revolution" has spawned an army of "knowledge workers" equipped with "intellectual property" ready to do battle in today's "information on demand" market. As a result, there is an ever-increasing need for applications and associated infrastructure to be up and available when the customer requires them, and to keep the critical supply of information flowing. It is for this reason that your business needs to have the delivery of its IT services organized and resourced to meet the current business requirements, and at the same time be flexible enough to be able to change with the same frequency and velocity that the business does.

For years, customers of IT computer services have long enjoyed the stability and predictability of centralized legacy mainframe applications. Most of their interactions with systems were through straightforward, unsophisticated, character-based screens, which essentially reflected a relatively simple single-threaded work process. Uncomplicated data structures served as the solid foundation on which the well-established custom application would reliably "chug" along. Database and system administrators lived a pretty uneventful existence, given the maturity of not only the application and hardware, but also the monitoring and maintenance tools.

In the scheme of things, it is really only recently that large-scale enterprise resource planning (ERP) applications, residing on a distributed UNIX environment with sophisticated front-ends served by PC-based servers and workstations, have really begun their assault on the mainframe market. Commercial off-the-shelf (COTS) ERP packages are becoming commonplace and more and more appear to be among the strategy of major industries. With the systems trend moving in this direction, IT operations have turned their attention to the infrastructure required, both environment and support structure, to deliver the level of service to which the customer base has become accustomed.

Having had the experience of little information and benchmarking from which to draw, it seemed to make sense that we put pen to paper, or more appropriately finger to keyboard. Our goal was simple: to document and share our findings, and more importantly, share the process we used to develop an integrated service delivery (ISD) model. *IT Services: Costs, Metrics, Benchmarking, and Marketing* was written to address the issues and challenges surrounding the development and implementation of an enterprise-wide operations center for application software. It's no mystery, if you are able to clearly define your end state, where you want to be, and if you have a "map" clearly marked with how to get there, and you have the resources and the means, then you will successfully make the "trip!" This book is your "map" to successfully developing, implementing, and measuring an ISD model.

As you progress through the book you will see that there are no "magic formulas" or proprietary methodologies, just a straightforward, organized, customer-oriented approach. The key being customer-oriented. With technology so widespread and readily available, competitive advantage must be sought through other avenues. These days a main competitive advantage comes through customer care and satisfaction. Think about your last PC shopping experience. In your search you probably noticed that PCs, for the most part, are essentially all the same. What factors went into your choice? After-sale support and service, 800 number ease of use, onsite repair versus depot or mail-in repair? All of these are customer-related factors. It is for this reason that we took a customer approach in developing our ISD model. Whether it is PCs, appliances, cars, or computing operations services, customers all want to be "handled with care." Using a ground-up approach, we modeled the services required and expected by our customer base, and it was from this base set of services that we developed and defined the entire ISD model. An approach that is implemented, is working, and is proven!

Here is a brief overview of what is contained within the book:

- Chapter 1 frames the book by describing the background and the reason for developing an integrated service delivery model. This chapter basically puts the book in perspective and gives you a frame of reference.

- Chapters 2 and 3 provide the detailed steps necessary to get started—from writing the "job ticket" and "charting the approach" to organizing the project and management teams.
- Chapters 4 and 5 describe the business linkages from a services and services framework perspective while defining the marketing and communication aspects of service development and delivery.
- Chapters 6 and 7 describe the development of requirements and the service model from a customer perspective. The chapters further detail how to develop the processes necessary to deliver the service model to the defined level of service.
- Chapters 8 and 9 detail how to structure the organization to deliver the service model, as well as how to develop a correlating resource and cost model.
- Chapters 10 and 11 walk you through the benchmarking process, help you to define the metrics against which you should measure your ISD delivery, and define how you know when you reach success.
- Chapters 12 and 13 review lessons learned and "key messages" along with the answers to frequently asked questions.

▶ ## Who Should Read This Book?

IT Services: Costs, Metrics, Benchmarking, and Marketing was written to be viewed from multiple perspectives: the IT professional, the business manager, the customer, and the student.

It serves as a "road map" for IT executives, IT managers, and IT senior technical personnel who are tackling the issues surrounding the development and implementation of an enterprise-wide operations center for commercial off-the-shelf (COTS) application software.

It is a practical guide for business managers working with the IT community to develop a stable, predictable, cost-effective support infrastructure for COTS application software supporting the enterprise.

It is an educational vehicle to help customers better understand what they should expect from their COTS application software support infrastructure and to be better able to articulate their requirements.

It is also an educational vehicle that provides the student, the aspiring IT and business professional, with a real-life practical application of developing and implementing an integrated service delivery model. Practical, not just theory.

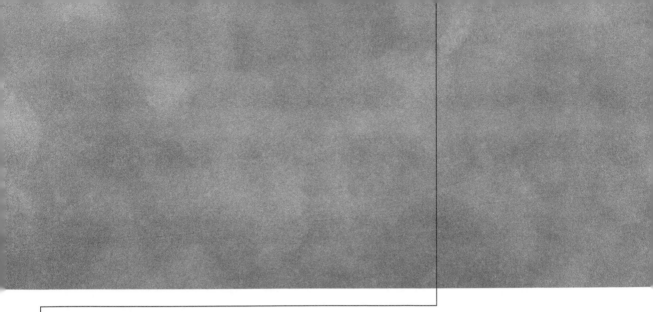

Acknowledgments

Thanks to Harris Kern for his tremendous input, help, and guidance throughout this whole process.

Thanks to Pat Cusick and Andy Kennedy for their input and encouragement.

Thanks to Bill Hanna for his valuable knowledge, input, and guidance.

Thanks to Stan Segal and Dane Nash for their support and encouragement.

Thanks to the Sun Professional Services Staff, especially Gerry Hedlund, Steve Evans, and Jefre Futch, for providing the foundation on which to build a service structure.

Thanks to Jeff Harris for his vast contacts and persistent follow-through.

Thanks to Marianne Conlon for her input.

Thanks to the Xerox teams who helped develop and implement the processes used in the ISD organization.

A very special thank you to the Xerox System Administration, Database Administration, Help Desk, and Oracle SA teams for making ISD a reality. Your persistent teamwork, dedicated work practices, and constant drive to improve the process have made ISD a success in Xerox and have greatly improved the level of service to our customers!

Finally, thank you to Deanna, Jennifer, and Brenda—we couldn't ask for three more supportive wives.

Introduction

Do you find that operations support in global distributed environments today almost completely rely on a few key senior support personnel coupled with a certain amount of heroics? Do you find that the operations staff tends to be in a reactive position as opposed to that of a proactive one? Do you find that you are struggling with folding your third-party support providers into the overall operations framework?

Let's face it, operations in a global distributed environment is, relatively speaking, a new paradigm. Challenges exist with being able to clearly define the technical environment along with its associated portfolio of services. Few benchmarks exist to use as a guide for setting up a successful operation. There is no point in having the best network, or the best applications, or the best servers in the world if your users cannot use them to build the business.

Management, pushed to deliver increased productivity and new sources of competitive advantage, increasingly rely on the availability of information systems as a contributing factor to user productivity.

Users, empowered by the influx of information to their desktop, are becoming more technologically savvy and more demanding about the capabilities and performance they need from their systems.

This means that greater focus needs to be placed on making sure information systems are accessible anytime to anyone who needs them. Equally important is to ensure that users are trained properly to make full use of and gain maximum productivity from these systems.

1

This book presents an enterprise integrated service delivery approach, that solves the problems of today's operations in global distributed environments by defining the scope of services and responsibilities that are a critical part of enterprise IT. The mission of integrated service delivery is to provide services and information that help users become even more productive.

This book focuses on the basic vision, processes, goals, and performance measures of an enterprise integrated service delivery operation, without limiting it to any particular delivery organization: internal or external, in-house, or outsourced. Learn how to set stretching goals, define a measurable set of services, and how to commit to delivering concrete benefits to the business!

1.1 Background

When we set out to develop an integrated service delivery (ISD) model to support a global distributed environment, little did we realize that the real power would be unleashed through tight integration, both from a services portfolio perspective as well as organizationally. It was only when we had finished defining our "customer requirements" and "benchmarking" (really more comparing and sharing than benchmarking), that we fully understood the keys to operational success.

We found that organizations, whether they were outsourced or not, were all experiencing similar trends: sagging levels of service (LOS) and rapidly increasing costs, both resulting in customer satisfaction woes. A common theme became fast apparent: the speed at which the business moved to a distributed environment, and associated application set, far outpaced the ability to manage them effectively, (see Figure 1–1).

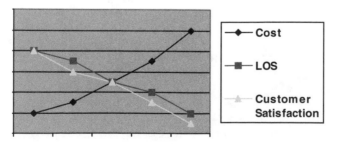

Figure 1–1   ISD trends.

It all points back to the fact that operations in a global distributed environment, being a new paradigm, is really only just maturing. Few benchmarks exist to use as a guide for setting up a successful operation, especially in larger organizations. In addition to not having "benchmark" organizations to model your operation, the appropriate technical tools do not exist to aid you in your quest to provide timely quality services at a manageable cost. Only now are the appropriate technical tools starting to become available.

Most of the frustrations associated with managing in this new paradigm stem from the successes that are enjoyed in the very stable legacy world. Legacy environments are normally predictable and centrally managed, and have had the benefit of 25 to 30 years of evolution and maturity, which makes them easily understood and managed. Variability drives change, change drives instability, and instability drives breakage, which drives cost and downtime, resulting in customer dissatisfaction. Those companies that have outsourced the operations of their distributed environments experience even further frustrations because this variability and instability only serves to decrease the ability of the service provider to respond to customer requirements in a timely fashion and usually translates into higher costs for the customer.

You are, however, not powerless in this world of ISD. We will show you ways to define your portfolio of services, and how to organize yourself to successfully deliver these services predictably, efficiently, and cost-effectively.

1.2 Sourcing from Within—Why Insource?

Interestingly enough, the companies that we visited in our quest for that all-elusive benchmark were all struggling with the outsourcing issue. Some companies had outsourced their entire operations piece and were struggling with the trends of decreasing LOS and increasing costs, as described earlier. Other companies were looking to outsource, citing that hardware and software operations were not a core competency. In either case, it is obvious that outsourcing is on everyone's mind and will continue to be a viable alternative. The point we do want to drive home is that even though it is a viable option, it is only the correct one if certain factors are met. However, unless you have truly defined and stabilized your requirements as well as your operation, you must lean toward insourcing.

There are many factors that come into play when deciding whether or not to outsource a specific functional area or business. There are entire books dedicated to this subject that go into much further detail than will be addressed in this chapter. It is, however, a very important piece of the overall ISD model, with regard to implementation, and will be addressed in this context.

Some of the more "important" factors to be considered are:

- Customer Satisfaction
- Financial Savings
- Delivery
- Quality
- Scalability
- Variability
- Measurability
- Predictability
- Definability
- Competency
- Staffing Capability/Retention
- Velocity (reaction to change
- Stability

As you can see, the decision to insource or outsource is not purely one of economic consideration; the ability to react to changes in the business with timely delivery of quality services and the Q and D of the quality, cost, delivery, and value (QCDV) equation, plays a very big role. QCDV, defined in detail in Chapter 5, plays a very big role in customer satisfaction, which is probably the biggest factor to consider. Therefore, in order to determine whether or not it makes sense to insource, it is important to understand what makes for a successful outsourcing partnership. The thought here is that if you cannot establish a successful partnership, then you should look to keep these services in-house.

Let's look a little deeper into a few of these factors and our rationale behind them:

1.2.1 Customer Satisfaction

This is the single most important factor to consider. You could argue that all the other factors listed above are a means to achieving customer satisfaction. This is why you see the list beginning and ending with customer satisfaction. To emphasize the point: How many times have you been willing to pay more for a good or a service because your level of satisfaction was so high? If the customer is not satisfied with the goods or services you provide, you can be sure they will either be looking elsewhere or escalating their concerns. It is for this reason that you must take a customer approach.

1.2.2 Definability and Measurability

Key factors to successfully outsource a specific functional area or business is dependent upon not only how well you define your customer requirements, but how well you can measure how they are being met. This may sound pretty basic and somewhat obvious; however, the fact remains that if you cannot clearly define what you need and are unable to put the appropriate measurements in place, then how can you expect your outsourcing partner to meet, let alone exceed, customer expectation? It cannot be stressed enough that you must be able to put the appropriate metrics in place. In addition to measuring your outsource partner, it allows your outsource partner the ability to measure themselves and to be proactive.

1.2.3 Stability and Variability

These, too, are among the most important factors to consider. Some of the most successful outsourcing ventures are with pieces of the business that are very stable, mature, definable, and measurable. This is why legacy operations are a perfect example of how to be successful with outsourcing. Legacy operations usually have very little variability associated with them. When we say variability we refer to changing requirements, changing functionality, dynamic customer base, etc. As stated before, variability drives change, change drives instability, and instability drives breakage, which drives cost and downtime, resulting in customer dissatisfaction. Think about the different pieces of your operation; those with the least amount of variability are those that are most manageable both from a delivery and a financial perspective.

1.2.4 Predictability

Predictability of quality, delivery, and cost of service also has a direct effect on customer satisfaction. A perfect example of this is the fast food industry. How many times have you gone to your favorite fast food franchise expecting to get predictable quality, service, and price, regardless of the town in which you are. It is the same with any good or service: Customers expect predictability.

Other factors and observations to consider:

- You may be able to outsource specific functions or areas with the core competencies listed above, but what you cannot outsource is a common goal. The goals of any ISD organization should be to increase level of service and to reduce cost, both of which will increase customer satisfaction. These goals can conflict with those of an outsource partner whose main goal is to increase revenues. It must be treated as a partnership if success is to be achieved.
- Outsourcing has an increase in "formality" associated with it that manifests itself in the form of "red tape." Therefore, if your business requirements are changing frequently, the ability for your outsource partner to respond with the same velocity may be hindered.

The message that should be coming across is that outsourcing makes the most sense in an environment, business area, or set of services that is definable, stable, and measurable. If these factors are lacking, then your outsource partner will not be able to provide the timely delivery of quality and predictable services in a cost-effective manner. In addition, you can be assured that customer satisfaction will be negatively impacted. The appeal of insourcing is that it allows you to experience the day-to-day operation of your business to better define your portfolio of services, the metrics by which to measure the delivery of these services, and provide for a chance to stabilize the operation. Once these factors have been defined, then the issue of outsourcing can be revisited.

1.3   Planning for Success

Success is not something that just happens. In order to be achieved, success must be planned for. There are certain factors, principles, and disciplines that will have a direct effect on the success of the outcome:

- Understand and Define Your Problem Set
- Define Your Scope
- Establish Guiding Principles
- Make Fact-Based Decisions
- Benchmark
- Understand Your Goal/Define Your End State
- Establish Coalitions/Gain Buy-In
- Exercise Quality
- Develop a Plan and Stick To It

1.3.1   Understand and Define Your Problem Set

Common sense, right? You would be surprised at the number of teams who find themselves significantly down the road and cannot remember or clearly articulate what the problem set is or what they are trying to address. The problem set should be understood, well defined, and documented. If you cannot clearly articulate the problem set, I can almost guarantee that it is not understood or defined. If you don't know what your problems are, then you will not know where to focus your portfolio of services.

1.3.2   Define Your Scope

Defining scope is one of those activities that you may find yourself revisiting a few times before the end of the project. However, do not let this dissuade you from developing an initial scope upfront. As you uncover facts, review results from "benchmark" visits, and in general become educated in the ISD world, you will find yourself adjusting your scope to incorporate "new" services or aspects into your model, or removing some "old" ones. The scope will help keep you on track.

1.3.3 Establish Guiding Principles

It is essential to establish guiding principles as a team. They provide the framework by which the team will approach all strategy and problem solving. They give the team a common perspective, based on those principles that are most valued. To better understand their importance, it is best to illustrate with the following example:

- Maximize Customer Satisfaction
- Maximize Level of Service
- Optimize Cost
- Optimize for Scalability and Provide for Reusablility

Any output or decision should satisfy part or all of these criteria. Once the principles are agreed to, they should be referred to often, especially if the team is divided on a decision or direction to take.

1.3.4 Make Fact-Based Decisions

It is very easy to fall into the trap of making anecdotal-based decisions. It is human nature to yield to emotion, experience, "gut feel," and perception. You will find that if you gather, organize, and analyze the facts, the outcome may be surprisingly different from that originally predicted. This is why any decision or approach should be supported by sufficient data, not so much to be able to defend or explain your position, but to provide assurance that you have truly thought things through objectively. Objectivity is the key.

1.3.5 Benchmark

Much can be said for the benefits of benchmarking. Its main purpose is to provide an exemplar, a high "watermark," so to speak, after which you look to model your specific functional area or business. Two challenges exist with a successful benchmarking exercise. The first challenge is to effectively collect and organize benchmark data so that you are making an "apples to apples" comparison of the operations you are studying. This can be more easily facilitated by developing an outline of the information you are trying to gather and developing an associated "questionnaire" to help you in your efforts to be consistent in your fact collection. The second challenge is finding a business, similar to your business, which truly has what is considered a "benchmark" operation. The whole benchmarking process, along with these challenges, is addressed in detail in a later chapter.

1.3.6 Understand Your Goal/Define Your End State

You are probably thinking to yourself that is ridiculously obvious, and we did too when we started out. However, our fact-finding left us "swimming" in so much data that we really found ourselves thrashing about, and when you are "wading" around in this much data you can find yourself losing sight of where it is you are trying to get to. The message here is to not only understand your goal and define your end state, but to refer to it regularly, use it as a guide, and, most importantly, modify it if necessary. Knowing where you are going and where you want to be is more than half the battle.

1.3.7 Establish Coalitions/Gain Buy-In

Developing an ISD model is not without its challenges; however, once it is completed the real work begins: the work of selling the model and gaining concurrence from management. This is why establishing coalitions is so important: gain buy-in early on and continue to sell your ideas throughout the entire project life cycle. An approach we took was to actually pull the management team into the development of the proposal, therefore, it was tailored exactly to how they like to be sold to. Certainly not a new approach, but a very effective one. You will find that when it comes time for final sign-off to move forward it will be a rather simple event if you have done a good job of selling early on.

1.3.8 Exercise Quality

Total quality management—an 80s and early 90s concept, right? Wrong! You will find that throughout this entire book we will refer to over a dozen "quality tools" that we used to develop our overall ISD model. Quality really plays heavily into making fact-based decisions, root cause analysis, and in organizing your thoughts in general. It was the basis for most of our work processes and was integral in helping us achieve our ISD model. You will see specific examples of how we used quality tools in later chapters. We are happy to be able to say that quality is alive and well.

1.3.9 Develop a Plan and Stick To It

This book is not meant to be a Project Management 101 course; however, having said that, I do want to stress that it is very difficult to successfully deliver without a solid plan that is followed and updated continuously. Tenacity is probably the most important quality of a good project team.

Getting Started

▶ 2.1   Writing the Job Ticket—"The Ask"

The successful development of an integrated service delivery strategy begins and ends with a well-developed job ticket. There is no mystery to the job ticket, simply put, it is the problem set—it sets the scope and boundaries and defines the expected set of deliverables. The job ticket helps you to determine the skills mix of the team you will need to assemble, as well as, helps you to "chart the course" for the team. A well-crafted, clear, succinct job ticket will serve as a charter by which the team will measure its progress.

Let's explore the components of a job ticket:

- Problem Statement
- Purpose/Statement of Deliverables
- Scope/Boundaries
- Team Definitions

2.1.1 Problem Statement

This is exactly what it suggests; it simply means to define the problem, and yet formulating a problem statement is not always easy. Don't be quick to jump the gun with what you think the problem is, or you could be treating what turns out to be only a symptom. Don't get caught in the trap of prematurely deciding the route cause, this too can lead you down a wrong path. It is important, however, to understand all of the symptoms, which are the manifestations of whatever the root causes may be.

For example, in Chapter 1, we referred to a graph of sagging customer satisfaction, sagging Level of Service (LOS), and increasing costs with outsourced services:

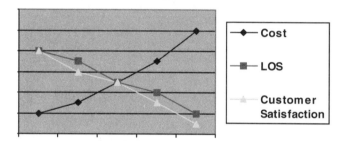

Figure 2–1   ISD trends.

Given that Figure 2–1 is a representation of symptoms experienced from an outsource partnership, there might be a tendency to have the problem statement read:

> Our outsource partner cannot deliver the required customer satisfaction, level of service, and required cost targets necessary to support a globally distributed environment.

It may not be immediately obvious, but this statement has a fundamental flaw. The way it is written implies a root cause; therefore, you may immediately focus your attention on potentially replacing your existing outsource partner, or on insourcing. These could both be very costly mistakes if your root causes lie in poorly defined requirements or a poorly defined portfolio of services. A more suitable problem statement might read:

The current infrastructure supporting our globally distributed environment is experiencing trends of sagging service levels and rapidly increasing costs, both resulting in customer satisfaction woes.

This statement makes no implications as to a root cause. It clearly defines the symptoms of the problem, keeping the focus fact-based. You can see the importance of clearly understanding and defining the problem statement.

2.1.2 Purpose/Statement of Deliverables

The purpose/statement of deliverables should tie directly to, and actually be a function of, the problem statement. They not only convey the expectations of the management team, including time frames for delivery, but they also serve as a framework for the team. To illustrate the point it is best to look at the following example:

The purpose of the team is to develop and provide alternatives to delivering an infrastructure that supports a globally distributed environment and provides a consistent and predictable level of service, increased customer satisfaction, and predictable and manageable costs. The final deliverable should be in the form of a proposal detailing each alternative, and have associated with it the relevant supporting facts, cost model, quality, and delivery metric impacts. The initial draft is to be delivered six weeks from the start of the project.

You can see from this example how the purpose is a direct function of the problem statement, and that the statement of deliverables is defined at a high level.

2.1.3 Scope/Boundaries

Boundaries serve multiple purposes. They provide a definition of scope and magnitude, and even more importantly, they define the limits of the team's empowerment. The team needs to understand the limits of their empowerment to affect change. For example, your company might be under a sole source agreement with a third-party vendor regarding certain aspects of your data center. This would clearly be out of scope and therefore a boundary would be set to protect this agreement. Given this, it is important to note that it is not always enough to define what is in scope, it is equally important to define what specifically is not in scope

Here is an example of a subset of scope/boundaries:

In Scope

- UNIX-based servers, hardware, software, and associate applications set.
- LAN networks within the walls of the data center on which the servers reside.
- Client software that supports the server-based application.
- Servers that reside in the Northeast region.
- Production, test, and development environments and associated servers.

Out of Scope

- The client itself and associated office productivity tools.
- The WAN outside of the data center.
- Mainframe servers and associated applications
- Application XYZ being supported by vendor UVW.

2.1.4 Team Definitions

In order to ensure the involvement, buy-in, and support across functions in the organization and across the corporation, it is important that a multitier team structure is put in place prior to the execution of the job ticket. The formation of the multitiered structure is essential to success.

1. The Core Team
    These are "the doers," the main team chartered to execute the job ticket. The team should be small, with broad yet diverse expertise. Its makeup should include members with the following skill sets: applications development and management, data

base administration, system administration, infrastructure development and management, and facilities management. These skills represent the essential components for a complete ISD model and therefore must be represented to ensure the appropriate coverage. It has been our experience that flexibility, dynamics, and velocity are in direct relationship to the size of the team.

2. Support Team

   The purpose of this team is really twofold: to provide guidance and/or a specific expertise to the core team, and to gain the buy-in of the middle management team through their involvement upfront. Therefore, the team should be made up of those IT managers who will be directly affected by the core team's out-put. The thought here is that by putting them on the team it will force interaction, allowing for their input to be included, and gaining their buy-in early.

3. Extended Support Team (if applicable)

   The formation of this team is really dependent on the size and structure of your company. Where it really adds value is when your IT Organization is organized by division with an overlying corporate IT. If this is the case, this should be a team from out-side the direct divisional IT organization. It is crucial to pull these people in to gain an expanded perspective, as well as for cross-corporate buy-in.

4. Steering Committee/Decision Team

   This is the team of direct decision makers who ultimately have authority over whether or not the proposal you will be present-ing will be approved. This is why gaining their buy-in early on in the project is so important.

 ## 2.2 Forming "The Core Team"

The formation of the core team is a relatively straightforward process. It all begins with selecting the right project manager and staffing the rest of the team with skilled dedicated resources.

2.2.1 Find a Strong /Capable Project Manager

As with any project, the strength and leadership of the project manager has a direct bearing on the success of the project team. Therefore, it is important that he or she possess certain core skills. First and foremost, for projects of this nature, it is important that the project manager be a "change agent," a tenacious proponent of change. This is a project with at times an insurmountable resistance to change, therefore it is necessary for the project manager to possess the skills necessary to break down barriers and to drive a new way to approach things. Equally important is the project manager's ability to build coalitions, influence, and sell. A team may have the greatest idea or approach, but if it cannot be clearly articulated, packaged, and sold, it will go nowhere.

2.2.2 Selecting the Members of the "Core Team"

Selecting the members of a team is normally a fairly uneventful task. Whoever is available or has the least amount "on their plate" is usually the obvious candidate for the team. However, given the importance of the task at hand, and given that the success of this team will be directly influenced by the varying skills of its team members, it is imperative to select each team based on the skills profile described earlier. To recap, the team's makeup should include members with the following skill sets: applications development and management, database administration, system administration, infrastructure development and management, and facilities management. Skill set is only one attribute to consider; equally important is attitude and delivery. As with the project manager, each team member must be an agent of change. They must possess a desire to deliver results amid much skepticism and resistance to change.

2.2.3 Staff Team with Dedicated Resources

Being part of this project team should not be a part-time job. Part-time resources result in conflicting priorities, sporadic delivery, and continuous review and "level up" across the team. To achieve a consistent cohesive strategy delivered with velocity, dedicated resources are imperative to success. Therefore, if you do extract a resource from another project or assignment, you should relieve that person completely of their commitments to that project or assignment. Distractions will ultimately affect the team's delivery in some fashion, whether it is through elongated delivery times, or worse, missed deliverables. If you cannot secure dedicated resources, then I would make the assertion that your management team does not see this project as a priority.

2.2.4 Empower the Work Group—Autonomy

If you are like most, when you hear the word empowerment you probably chuckle or roll your eyes, given that it has been a term often misused. The fact remains, however, that empowerment is key to the success of the team. You must, as a team, be given the latitude to define your approach and make the basic decisions necessary to deliver a cohesive and integrated solution, and that means being able to think out of the proverbial "box." Where empowerment can fall short is when management forms a team of this nature and simply says "you're empowered" and expects you to go forth and slay dragons in the name of progress. To truly get the most out of empowerment it is necessary to define the boundaries within which the team must operate, as well as communicate expectations. This all points back to the job ticket. In addition, it is necessary to establish a communication plan that includes a support team and decision team review and feedback process. Frequent review and feedback will become the team's critical factors for success. This will allow for quick feedback on decisions that the team made and the approach that the team is taking.

▶ 2.3   Charting the Approach

2.3.1   Restate the Problem Set

Given the importance of the problem statement, which serves as the "anchor point" of the entire project, it is necessary for the team to not only understand it but to be able to restate it in terms that do not easily allow for multiple interpretations. This is necessary for two main reasons. First, it is critically important that each member of the team share a common understanding of the problem they are trying to address, and by working through the exercise of restating it, it provides a vehicle through which this can be accomplished. It forces team leveling through an interactive discussion of each member's view of the problem. Second, restating the problem provides a detailed view of the problem in simple, straightforward terms, allowing for easy communication and little room for misunderstanding.

Let's use our problem statement from above as an example of restating the problem statement:

> The current infrastructure supporting our globally distributed environment is experiencing trends of sagging service levels and rapidly increasing costs, both resulting in customer satisfaction woes.

Restated, the problem set may look like this:

- Support personnel turnover is at 100%
- Server uptime is at 82%, 17% below agreed to level of service
- Network uptime is at 90%, 9% below agreed to level of service
- Portfolio of services limited and undocumented
- Service delivery inconsistent
- Ability to respond to new or changing requirements is not timely
- Workstation costs have increased 28% over the last three years
- Labor costs have increased 20% over the last two years
- Customer satisfaction surveys reflect a 68% satisfaction level, down 21% over the past three years

You can see that there is little room for interpretation as to what the "problems" are and where to focus.

2.3.2 Define the Scope

As with the problem statement, it is necessary to be clear about what is defined to be in and out of scope; therefore, using the scope and the boundaries defined in the "job ticket" as the guide, it is necessary to provide a very descriptive list. When defining the scope, you must also keep in mind any necessary time-dependent requirements you may be under. For example, a third-party contract may expire within a year, or you have a project that will be implemented in 18 months; therefore, you want to prioritize related requirements accordingly.

Depending on these types of "time-related" dependencies, along with depth and breadth of the job ticket, it might be necessary to phase your deliverables. This is where management's expectation gets set, so you want to make sure that your scope is not too broad that it is unachievable. Conversely, you want to ensure that it is not too narrow that you do not derive value from what you deliver. Remember the whole reason for your team's existence is to deliver results, so keep the scope manageable.

2.3.3 Define Your Work Process/ Review and Feedback Loop

When we refer to the work process we are really referring to how the team will operate within itself and how it will operate with the support and decision teams. Where some teams of this nature get into trouble is that they do not set up enough review and feedback sessions early enough. Frequent review and feedback will become the team's critical factors for success. Metaphorically speaking, each review and feedback session allows the team an opportunity to "right" or "steer" the ship to its final destination. Can you imagine if you were on a cross-country trip and you waited until you were only a mile away from your final destination before you asked for directions or consulted your map? Use the support and decision teams as part of your tool set, not as a gate or a milestone you must pass.

2.3.4 Gain Buy-In Early

Gaining buy-in early is something that is simple to accomplish and whose importance cannot be stressed enough. The actual sign-off on the proposal should be, relatively speaking, a mere formality if you have successfully gained early buy-in. The real key is to involve the support and decision teams throughout the entire life cycle of the project.

When people think of involvement they usually think of e-mail. They feel that if they create a distribution list (DL) and mail their latest documents out to the world then they have done their job of keeping everyone "involved." This is by no means the involvement referred to in this chapter. When we talk of "involvement" we refer to "bringing in," "solicitation of feedback," and "overcommunication." It is the team's responsibility to physically "bring in" the support teams and the decision team. Call meetings, review facts and findings, and most importantly, "solicit feedback." Draw upon the various team's experiences and expertise; after all, they have been put in place for this reason. Find ways to incorporate feedback into the team's output. There is no better way to gain buy-in than to use someone's input in the final output.

Lastly, do not be afraid to "overcommunicate." When referring to "overcommunication," it does not mean to inundate people with e-mail and voice mail. What it does refer to, however, is to schedule regular and frequent reviews of the team's progress and outputs. This will ensure that you are on track from the support team's and decision team's perspectives and will prevent you from potentially wasting a lot of time heading down the wrong path.

2.3.5 Have Fun!

Some of the most fulfilling project experiences occur on small, dedicated, "task force type" teams operating within a well-defined scope. Therefore, work hard, stay focused, "bring in," "solicit feedback," "overcommunicate," and HAVE FUN!

Establishing and Managing Coalitions—Gaining Buy-In

▶ 3.1 Establish Management Buy-In Early

Sign-off on the proposal does not occur the day it is presented to management. If you hope to gain sign-off, concurrence from the management team must occur well before the proposal is submitted for their final review. This concurrence can be easy if you establish management buy-in early on in the proposal development phase. It is important to keep the management team close to your progress through direct involvement in the way of a very strong communication and feedback loop.

Frequent proposal status and review meetings will ensure that you have management's buy-in as you progress through development. Be sure to solicit and incorporate each member's direct input even if you have to do it through one-on-one reviews. People are not inclined to reject a document that contains their own ideas; therefore, finding a way to get them involved is imperative.

Although it sounds pretty easy, gaining buy-in is not always straight-forward. Not everyone on the management team may share your objectives or your convictions; you need to assess and classify each member of the management team as either a supporter, a non-supporter, or "on the fence."

3.1.1 Supporter

Just because someone is a supporter does not mean you will get his or her support and sign-off by default. It does mean, however, that you should not have to expend much energy selling them conceptually. You do, however, still have to spend time soliciting their input and selling them on your approach.

3.1.2 Non-Supporter

A non-supporter will obviously be your most difficult challenge, because you must sell them both conceptually as well as on the overall approach. I wish there was some magic formula, but it is just not that simple—you will need to roll up your sleeves and work to gain their support. Experience shows that to gain this support, it is essential that you keep all outputs and discussions fact-based, and keep emotion out of the equation. If you keep the facts vague, and rely on "cheerlead-ing" and emotion, you run the risk of the non-supporter perceiving you as promoting an agenda. In addition, here is where seeking input and "overcommunicating" plays a big role. No matter what the out-come, do not become discouraged because you may not be able to ever sway the non-supporter your way, so best you can hope for is majority support.

3.1.3 "On the Fence"

People "on the fence" will generally behave in one of two ways. They will either be swayed by the majority opinion, or they will be swayed by a particular individual whom they deem as a subject matter expert or whose opinion they hold in high respect. Winning them over will rely on your ability to assess what type they are. In any case, this does not relieve you of the need to remain fact-based and to solicit input.

If you are able to successfully build coalitions and gain buy-in early, management sign-off should truly be nothing more than a formality. If you have any doubts about whether or not the proposal will be approved, then you probably have not kept the management team close enough.

3.2   Establish Customer Buy-In Early

Success begins and ends with customer satisfaction. The portfolio of services and associated cost models must be developed with the customer in mind and must align with the customer's goals and objectives, and satisfy their overall requirements. Simply put, you must take a customer approach. This is why we have dedicated a whole chapter to "Taking a Customer Approach."

With some exceptions, the majority of the customer's goals, objectives, and requirements can be anticipated for the most part. They require a larger offering of predictable, high-quality services delivered consistently and quickly, all for less money. With technology turning over every six months and the Internet and telecommunication "explosion," business has its hands full with keeping up with end-customer demands. These demands drive change and the business must be nimble enough to react to these changes. Consequently, the ISD operation must also be able to respond in turn. A lethargic operation will eventually impact the business to the point where they will be forced to consider other options (e.g., outsourcing, alternate vendors, etc.).

The best way to ensure that you align with your customer and gain their buy-in is by involving them early on in the development of the portfolio of services, associated cost model, and organization structure. This will ensure that the customer feels a part of the development of the ISD operation and will also feel certain accountability for its success.

3.3 Establish Supplier Coalitions

3.3.1 Procure Subject Matter Experts (SMEs)

Depending on the situation, you may or may not have at your disposal the subject matter experts necessary to develop an ISD model. For example, if your ISD delivery is currently outsourced to a third party, chances are you would not have redundant skills as this would most likely be cost-prohibitive. Or, if ISD delivery is a new requirement of your company or department, you may not yet have on staff the necessary subject matter experts required. In either case you will need to procure knowledgeable resources to staff the project team developing the ISD model and associated strategy.

As outlined in Chapter 2 "Getting Started," the team's makeup should include members with the following skill sets: applications development and management, database administration, system administration, infrastructure development and management, and facilities management. You need to assess what skills you currently have available to you, what skills you can secure within your company or department, and what skills you will need to go outside the company to augment the project team. If you are required to go outside the company, insist on resources that are not only SMEs, but also have a demonstrated and proven record of delivery. This may sound obvious, however, if you do not specifically ask for this and press your supplier, you will normally get the first person coming off billable assignment instead of the person that would most likely fit your requirements.

3.3.2 Test Market for Resource Availability— Can It Be Staffed Effectively?

You will find that one of the most challenging pieces of developing and implementing an ISD operation is the ability to understand the staffing requirements as well as the ability to staff those requirements effectively. Therefore, it is a good idea to test the market for resource availability as early as possible. The market in this case can be internal sources as well as external sources, including contracts, consultants, and "head-hunting" agencies. The real difficulty will be attempting to communicate your needs while you are still developing them. Because it is anticipated that resources will be difficult to secure, it is very important that you begin to test for availability as soon in the process as possible.

The first step to staffing effectively is to develop a detailed resource model. The resource and staffing model details the required skill sets necessary to satisfy the *work breakdown structure* and associated *services model*. The work breakdown structure, services model, and associated *resource model* will be covered in detail in subsequent chapters. However, I will briefly touch upon the resource since it plays an integral role in this discussion.

Without getting into much detail, essentially the staffing model gives you a quantitative and qualitative way to identify the resources necessary to successfully staff the work breakdown structure. Here in Table 3–1 is an example of a resource model:

Table 3–1   Resource Model

Service	Sched or On Dmnd	Offered	Skill Set	Freq	UOM
Cost Management 1.1.1	S	5x8	Senior Clerical	260	Days
Maintain charge-back model					
Ensure new transfer agreements in place					
Renew yearly transfer agreements					
Ensure revenue received from customers					
Cost reporting to customer and management					
LOS Management 1.1.2	S	5x8	Mgr	260	Days
Management of level of service agreements					
Tracking of LOS					
Execution of LOS					
Reporting of LOS					
Conduct service level reviews					
Conduct customer satisfaction survey					
Maintain a service improvement plan					
Maintain a service publication					
Project Management 1.1.3	D	5x8	Mgr	5	Days
Customer engagement					
Requirements gathering and documentation					
Service delivery coordinator					

Table 3–1 Resource Model (Continued)

Service	Sched or On Dmnd	Offered	Skill Set	Freq	UOM
Server Performance Tuning 1.2.1.1	O/D	**24x7 Pager**	**SA**	365	Days
Response to help desk call on poor performance					
Maintain history information on server performance					
Make adjustments to UNIX level system parameters					
Compile database statistics					
Make adjustments to database for performance					
Compile network performance metrics					
Follow change control					
Server monitoring and corrective action 1.2.1.2	O/D	**24x7 Pager**	**SA**	365	Days
Connectivity from outside servers alive and well					
Disk drive capacity with defined limits					
Network connectivity alive and well					
Paging software active					
No runaway processes					
Memory utilization within defined limits					
Ensure all databases active after backup process					
Detect problems or bottlenecks					
Analyze performance compared to capacity					
Provide tier II server level support					
Troubleshoot database problems					
Software event monitoring					
System fault detection					
Disk fault detection					
Print Services 1.2.1.3	O/D	**24x7 Pager**	**SA**	260	Days
Troubleshooting in the decentralized environment					
Black box hookups					
Software installation/configuration on new printers					
File server management of print queues					
Resolve printing problems					
Ongoing DB monitoring and maintenance 1.2.1.4	S	**24x7 Pager**	**Junior DBA**	60	DBs
Database activity					
Concurrent manager activity					
ORASRV process alive and well					
Listener server alive and well					
Monitor for down databases					
Monitor for down concurrent managers					

You will notice that the resource model is driven directly off the service model and defines the skills and effort necessary to deliver the services described. As you progress on the resource modeling you begin to get an idea of the types of resources you will require, and equally important, the quantity of those resources.

Obviously, a fully developed resource model comes well into the project and will not be available upfront. However, even though this model is not completed, it does begin to give you an idea of the types of resources you will require to successfully staff the work breakdown structure. Once you start to get a picture of the types of resources you require, you can begin to develop a *skills matrix* (see Table 3–2).

Table 3–2   Skills Matrix

SA	OSA	DBA	Clerical	Network	Manager
Junior SA	Junior OSA	Junior DBA	Clerical	Network Specialist	Technical Manager
SA	OSA	DBA	Senior Clerical		Manager
Senior SA	Senior OSA	Senior DBA			Senior Manager

The skills matrix is what you will need to begin to engage resource suppliers (e.g., human resources, contract agencies, consultants, headhunters, etc.). This is important because it will allow you to begin to test the market for resource availability. I cannot stress the importance of starting this process as early as possible. As stated earlier, staffing will be one of the most challenging exercises and the most critical. If you cannot staff with qualified competent resources you can be assured of not meeting the level of service. Staffing is a critical measure of success!

Once you develop a relationship with your resource suppliers you can pull them in as part of the extended team, and as you develop and expand the resource model and associated skills matrix they can plan and react in a timely manner to your overall requirements. It's all about establishing and building coalitions as early as possible in the cycle.

▶ 3.4   Establish an Information Network

As you develop and build coalitions with the decision team, extended team, internal departments and suppliers, and external suppliers, you, in essence, are establishing the basis of an "information network." The information network will become an excellent tool for gathering, sharing, and disseminating information instrumental in developing the

ISD model and strategy. Once you establish a relationship, the only thing between how closely you want them tied to the project and how closely they feel tied to the project is the quantity and types of information being shared with them, as well as the frequency of communication.

At the risk of sounding redundant, overcommunicate. Keep the flow of information open and turn any feedback around as quickly as practical. This accomplishes a few things. It reinforces that any and all feedback is considered and valued, therefore making those that have contributed feel even more closely tied to the output from the project team. It also keeps everyone "up to speed" on the latest information, reducing the need to provide "level-up" sessions. You will reap many benefits through continuous evolution and refinement of a strong information network.

3.5 Identify and Understand Risk

Let's face it, risk can never be completely removed, and it exists in some form in every project or venture you embark on. You can, however, plan for and reduce your exposure to risk. The only way to minimize risk is to first identify what the risks are, and understand their effects on reaching the goals of the project.

For example, let's use ISD model resourcing as a risk. As we stated earlier in this chapter, staffing the ISD model will be one of your biggest challenges. If we did not identify this risk upfront and begin to engage various resource suppliers early on, you might have an excellent strategy that has been approved and funded by management only to find out that you cannot successfully deliver it. However, by identifying and understanding this risk early on, you can plan to minimize the risk upfront in the development of the ISD model. In addition, management can be made aware of the pending risk, and can drive a more fact-based decision on whether or not the risk is too great to proceed forward.

Keep a list of risks and associated countermeasures up to date and visible to the information network!

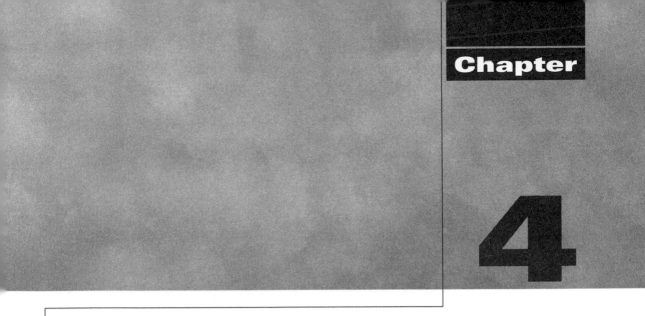

Business Linkage

Services do not exist in a vacuum. They do not spontaneously appear for no reason, or if they do, their existence may point to a significant business problem. Being able to identify and understand the relationship between the business and the services that are ultimately supplied at the end of the service pipeline is critical. This may be a very deliberate exercise or may be more intuitive as in the case this book uses as the primary reference.

▶ 4.1   Understanding the Company Mission

Most companies have a mission statement that often reflects executive management's vision of the business's direction and goals. There is an old proverb that states where there is no vision there is no hope (Proverbs 29:18). The mission statement cannot stand on its own unless it is meant only as a public relation or marketing gambit rather than a key point to link goals and objectives to. In the realm of psychology, the term "identity" relates to the basic sense of self, the core of values and mission in life. The absence of a well-formed personal identity can often lead to major psychological problems, or, at a minimum, limit the individual's ability to reach their full potential. In the business world enterprises must likewise have a defined and communicated identity or mission that will form the basis for developing strategies and serve as the guiding beacon and key navigational tool for the enterprise. Without this foundation, any operating framework and architecture, including the service delivery framework, will not be well formed. The absence of a clearly defined and communicated identity or mission can be potentially disastrous to any enterprise.

In the past the definition of an enterprise's identity or mission has been decreed by an autocratic CEO, or created through a collaborative process involving varying organizational levels and participants. Traditionally, once the identity or mission was established, it remained unchanged, often for the lifetime of the enterprise.

A space rocket off target a fraction of an inch at launch will miss its target by orders of magnitude if corrections are not made during the course of its flight. It is critical for business enterprises to be on target with their missions. It is also vital to realize that just as with the rocket, substantial energy must be expended to change course settings or missions in midstream. Just as not having a well-formed and communicated mission can be fiscally disastrous for an enterprise, not having the ability to validate the mission, measure adherence to it, and make required adjustments can be equally disastrous.

The traditional approach of assuming the mission as valid and often using it as a public relations slogan rather than a guiding force to be actively measured against will not work in an environment in which change occurs at exponential rates. A new approach to the strategic business view must be developed to not only accommodate this change, but also embrace it and use it as a competitive advantage.

Only with a thorough understanding of the overall enterprise mission, direction, and dynamics can an ISD environment truly be created.

4.2 Services in a Traditional Business Framework

Services must be structured within the IT organization in order to deliver them in the most efficient and effective manner. Integrated services also exist within a business framework and must support and facilitate vertical, horizontal, and logical business linkages.

The traditional approach to establishing enterprise direction was to create a mission or purpose statement along with supporting strategies. Once these were in place, goals and objectives were defined to accomplish the strategies, and finally tactical/operational plans were developed and executed in accordance with the strategic direction. One of the operational plans that was usually, but not always, created was the IT plan.

Figure 4–1 represents a traditional approach leading to an IT plan that would normally contain the service portfolio to be offered to the enterprise.

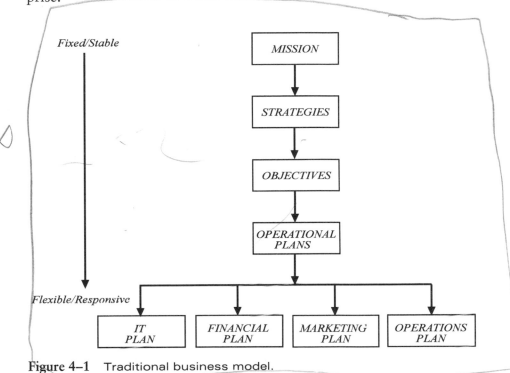

Figure 4–1   Traditional business model.

As indicated above, the traditional approach to planning is sequential in nature and generally very stable or almost fixed at the top of the hierarchy, becoming more flexible or responsive to change as the process moves downward. Once this sequence was completed and documented, usually on an annual basis, the product generally occupied a prominent position on bookshelves. Only at year-end was the product of this process usually accessed again. At this time, traditional heroes are identified for bonuses and martyrs designated to assume blame. There may or may not be any linkage, communication, or coordination between the various plans or in their implementation. In many instances each plan represented a departmental silo that only operated in that realm. The services that flowed out of these silos often did not support the enterprise mission or optimize IT resources.

Communicating the enterprise direction was often stymied by bottle-necks at various organizational levels or not communicated at all. In the absence of a clear, coordinated and communicated direction, several "assumed" directions drove the planning and execution of the enterprise's functions. This lack of effective process reduces the ability to focus staff resources appropriately and defuses technology's capability to leverage resources, support targeted growth, and enable innovation. Services delivered are often substantially off target due in part to this "noise" in the communication of the enterprise direction.

The IT plan is generally segregated into two major components: application services and operations services. The elements in each of these components can vary depending on organizational philosophy and enterprise-specific requirements. Interestingly, an element of the ISD coming from operations services will entail providing support for application services.

The traditional approach described above is the most prevalent model in use today. Even when it is used religiously, which is not common, the traditional sequentially oriented framework does not provide for sufficient responsiveness and flexibility to support an effective ISD in the current business environment. The explosively rapidly changing business climate requires a totally new ISD framework.

4.3   Object-Oriented Service Delivery Framework

It seems only fair that since everything else in IT these days is object-oriented, services should be as well. The same attributes that exist in object-oriented programming and languages should also be applied to services.

While the traditional approach to directing an enterprise assumed the mission was relatively fixed, in actuality, it was changing. Much like the molecules in an apparently solid object are in constant motion, the mission, strategies, objectives, and plans of the enterprise are also in motion. The mission or purpose of the enterprise is always being impacted, sometimes very slowly and in minute increments, and sometimes very rapidly and in orders of magnitude. In the object-oriented framework the mission is represented as a super class in a strategic enterprise framework that defines the identity of the enterprise as "Big Rules." Subclasses of the "Big Rules," or business rules, inherit the attributes of the mission and form the equivalent to the strategies and objectives in the traditional framework. The strategic enterprise framework provides the foundation for business domains to reside. One of the business domains is the IT domain.

The stimulus for the changes to the mission or strategic enterprise framework can originate externally in the form of technological innovations, economic occurrences, industry shifts, or political affairs. The stimulus can also be from within in the form of reorganizations, new products, or financial constraints. An external environment interface must exist and be plugged into the strategic enterprise framework to ensure that information can flow effectively through all components of the strategic framework, as shown in Figure 4–2.

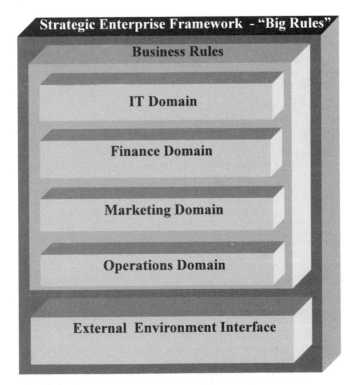

Figure 4–2   The strategic framework flow.

The business domains contain business objects that can be independent or joined to form components that must exist in order for the strategies to be satisfied. Business event utilization must be planned, sequenced, and executed to complete the accomplishment of a segment of the enterprise's mission.

Within the business domains or object classes are subclasses that, in the case of the IT domain, represent services. Each of these services are composed of three elements: people, technology, and process (see Figure 4–3).

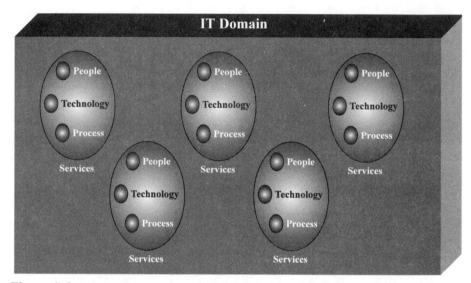

Figure 4–3 Business domain subclasses.

The strategic enterprise framework in today's world must communicate with external stimuli, pass its definition to business domains, validate itself periodically, and redefine itself if required. The enterprise must understand the financial, cultural, and organizational impact of reinventing itself. Not having the capabilities or methods to measure the need for change and enable even continuous reinvention can create major problems in today's rapidly changing global environment.

Strategies, objectives, and plans all must have the ability to share or communicate necessary information with each other, restrict or hide inappropriate information, and ensure that the essential common denominators of people, process, and technology are factored into each model component or object.

Chapter **4** I Business Linkage

By constructing services in an object-oriented fashion, they will be able to move within the IT organization. The services will still be able to link to other services while retaining the skill, technology, and process attributes necessary to deliver the appropriate output given their environmental circumstances. This object-oriented framework produces a truly ISD capability.

▶ 4.4   Balancing the Services

Services that are focused on supporting the "squeakiest wheel" in the organization may not be optimizing the resources in the IT organization or leveraging the most valuable business contributors. Traditionally, if the top executive has a finance background the entire organization, including IT, will have a tendency to expend more energy on financially oriented activities such as cost control. In the same vein, if the top executive comes from a marketing background the organizational focus will most likely be revenue generation. Insuring that the organization views its responsibilities in a balanced manner requires a discipline that should be applied throughout the enterprise, including the IT function.

Services that the IT function provides the enterprise must support the balanced needs of the entire organization. One method of ensuring that this happens is through the use of the balanced scorecard approach.

The balanced scorecard approach is an approach that first burst on the scene with a *Harvard Business Review* article, "The Balanced Scorecard—Measures that Drive Performance," January–February 1992, written by David Norton and Robert S. Kaplan. Since that article, the methodology has become widely accepted as an extremely valuable tool to ensure that strategies address all areas of the enterprise, and has become a core management process to ensure that resources are allocated appropriately to the support of the strategies.

The balanced scorecard methodology, in addition to providing discipline to ensure all facets of the enterprise are viewed in a balanced manner, provides an architecture that includes measurement of goal accomplishments that grow out of the methodology.

The balanced scorecard methodology forces all aspects of the enterprise to be viewed from four different perspectives:

- Financial Perspective
- Customer Perspective
- Internal-Business Process Perspective
- Learning and Growth Perspective

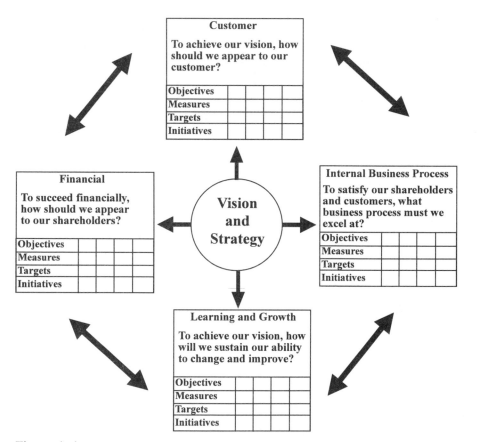

Figure 4–4   The balanced scorecard framework. (*Adapted and reprinted by permission of* Harvard Business Review. *Excerpt from "Using The Balanced Scorecard as a Strategic Management System" by Robert S. Kaplan and David P. Norton, (January–February 1996). Copyright 1996 by the President and Fellows of Harvard College, all rights reserved.*)

The financial perspective looks at strategies, goals, and services from a stockholder and CFO's standpoint.

The customer perspective looks at strategies, goals, and services from a customer satisfaction, marketing, and pricing standpoint.

The internal-business process perspective looks at strategies, goals, and services from a production, quality, and service standpoint.

The learning and growth perspective looks at strategies, goals, and services from the standpoint of how well an organization accommodates change, learns from its mistakes, and develops its resources.

Figure 4–4 provides an overview of the balanced scorecard framework. The companies that utilize this methodology have an excellent tool to ensure that all the enterprises' objectives and initiatives are adequately supported by services. Another valuable use of the methodology is in the area of measurement. Not only do services need to be balanced across the enterprise to ensure that adequate coverage is provided, but the level of service and the resources required also need to be balanced. Measures in the different balanced scorecard perspectives can be linked to service level agreements at the operations level. Examples of business measures in the methodology are:

Financial Perspective

- Return on Investment
- Economic Value Added
- Revenue/Employee
- Unit/Costs

Customer Perspective

- Customer Satisfaction
- Market Share
- Customer Retention

Internal-Business Process Perspective

- Quality
- Response Time
- New Product Sales Percentage

Learning and Growth Perspective

- Employee Satisfaction
- Reskilling Capabilities
- Team Alignment and Performance

The investment to create a balanced scorecard framework and surround it with management processes is not trivial. However, there is software that provides support for this investment.

▶ 4.5 Services Linkages

Vertically linking services to the business mission can be adequately addressed in the traditional hierarchical approach described above. The more complex object-oriented approach covered how services can be linked in multiple directions, again described above. Since services do not exist in a static state, the logical flow of the services is another view that must be addressed if the ISD concept is to be successfully executed.

The ability to link and trace each service delivered in an ISD program to enterprise goals and objectives and, ultimately, the mission itself, is key to being able to justify and, if necessary, defend resources utilized to deliver the services. Whether the linkage from the services to the mission is traditional hierarchical, modular, or object-oriented, relationships should be established and documented.

The ability for an IT executive to be able to directly and straightforwardly link the services his operation produces to the business element the service supports can be the key to survival for the service and, perhaps, the executive. Additionally, by being able to link the mission and the services that support its accomplishment, the communication of the enterprise's direction and path is made easier. When service providers have a clear understanding of how the work they are performing contributes to the enterprise as a whole, their tasks can be much more fulfilling.

Linking all enterprise activities, especially services, to a single mission provides a very powerful synergistic effect. It "puts a lot of wood behind the arrow."

The logical linkage of services takes the form of a flow of services that begins with the request for service and is fulfilled in a complete cycle of service delivery, validation of completion/completeness/quality, and an examination for service improvement opportunities.

Figure 4–5 depicts a basic flow or logical linkage of services.

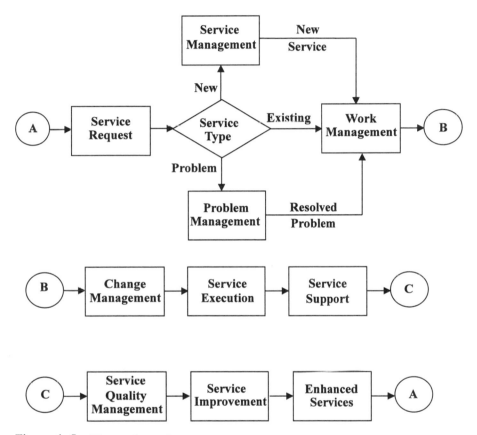

Figure 4–5 Flow of services.

The flow of services begins with the initial request flowing directly to a work management function to initiate provisioning of the service for existing services. In the event there is no existing service, service management creates a new service or if the initial request relates to a problem, problem management researches and resolves the problem and passes the services request to work management.

Change management performs an impact analysis and passes the request to service execution to perform the actual work, which is supported after execution by support management.

Quality management validates that the customer is satisfied with the service. If not satisfied, it passes the request to service improvement, for a continious improvement check, and creates an enhanced service, if appropriate.

This very simplified service flow represents a logical sequence of events that occur when a service is requested and is delivered in an ISD approach.

The ability to link the activities that comprise services to the business enterprise horizontally, vertically, and logically, will directly affect the value the enterprise will derive from their investment in IT.

Understanding the company mission, the framework, or context the integrated services will be delivered in, and how they should be balanced and linked, are key precursors to initiating the actual initial thrust of discovering the service requirements. As mentioned in the opening statement of this section, how deliberate and specific this exercise is will vary from firm to firm. The more the leaders of the effort have internalized the mission and direction of the enterprise the less deliberate the exercise needs to be.

Marketing and Communications

Understanding the company's mission, its linkage with the IT functions, and how the task of determining and defining the services will be initiated, is essential to delivering a set of integrated enterprise services. Gaining early support from all the key stakeholders is another requirement for success. The most basic and essential prerequisite to marketing and communicating the IT story is having a history of delivering quality, cost-effective, valuable services on a timely basis. Given that these vital initiatives are accomplished, marketing and communicating of the product, and delivery of integrated enterprise services, is critical to ensure that maximum organizational benefit and return on IT investment is achieved.

A Gartner Research note, "Marketing the IS Organization: Questions and Answers," published 26 September 1996, defines marketing from an IT perspective:

> Marketing is essentially the process of understanding, anticipating, shaping, and satisfying the customer's perception of value. For the IT organization, marketing entails knowing the primary internal markets; enterprise executives, operation and line managers, work-area managers, and production end users investigating and predicting their requirements,

41

developing feedback mechanisms for performance, and articulating services relevant to the internal group's ideas of value. For example, marketing to enterprise executives should focus on governance issues (e.g., decision making, funding, metrics, and architecture), whereas marketing to business managers should focus on the changes and possibilities caused by IT's impact on business and the business's impact on IT. (Reprinted with permission—August 1999.)[1]

Success of an IT organization depends on its operational capabilities, but it must leverage those capabilities with a persuasive, politically savvy, marketing and communication approach that is ingrained in the culture of the organization.

▶ 5.1 Marketing 101

5.1.1 Identify and Define the Product/Service

Chapter 6, "Taking a Customer Approach," speaks to the process of determining what services should be offered to support a targeted business environment. Defining the IT services in business terms and their impact on the business's operational ability to deliver the expected service to their customer is another view of the same entity.

While the descriptions of the deliverables in Table 5–1 may be understandable to some faction of the business constituency, they do not generally reflect an understanding of the business initiatives they are supporting or enabling.

---

1. D. Turick, "Marketing the IS Organization: Questions and Answers," GartnerGroup Research Note, September 26, 1996.

Table 5–1 Delivery of IT Services from an IT Perspective

IT Services	IT Deliverables
Server monitoring and corrective action 1. Tier II Level Support 2. Internal & External Connectivity Monitoring 3. DB Activity Monitoring 4. Capacity/Utilization/Performance Monitoring 5. Process Execution Monitoring 6. Day of Operations Troubleshooting 7. Day of Operations Problem Resolution	The deliverables that will be generated out of these services are continuous monitoring, tracking of the primary systems processes, and supporting computing infrastructure to meet the requirements of the business unit as well as on-demand user service requests. Fault detection will result in proactive reporting to the proper support organizations. Operations will provide Tier II corrective action to maintain the service level requirements.
Print Services 1. Hardware/Software Installation & Configuration 2. Print Queue & Spooling Management 3. Secured Printing Management 4. Printing Problem Troubleshooting and Resolution	The deliverables that will be generated out of these services include: requirements specifications, physical, logical and network configurations, equipment orders, installation work orders, and documentation updates.
Network Management 1. Network Capacity Planning 2. Network Topology Documentation 3. Network Load/Impact Analysis 4. Modem Connection Setup and Access 5. New Network Connectivity Mgt 6. Naming Services Conflict Resolution	The deliverables that will be generated out of these services include capacity and performance requirements, network configurations, telco coordination, intranet coordination, installation work orders, and documentation updates.

The deliverables described in Table 5–2 are in more generic business terms. To the extent that an IT organization can identify specific business unit objectives and goals that can be supported by these services and plugged into the deliverables section, the likelihood is that the deliverables will not only be better understood, but internalized and supported as well.

Table 5–2 The Same Service Deliverables Viewed from a Business Perspective

IT Services	Business Deliverables
Server monitoring and corrective action 1. Tier II Level Support 2. Internal & External Connectivity Monitoring 3. DB Activity Monitoring 4. Capacity/Utilization/Performance Monitoring 5. Process Execution Monitoring 6. Day of Operations Troubleshooting 7. Day of Operations Problem Resolution	The deliverables that will be generated out of these services are at a consistent high level of operational service, per the agreed to service level, on an ongoing basis, and the rapid proactive addressing of any potential problem that could interrupt that service.
Print Services 1. Hardware/Software Installation & Configuration 2. Print Queue & Spooling Management 3. Secured Printing Management 4. Printing Problem Troubleshooting and Resolution	The deliverables that will be generated out of these services include the installation, deployment, daily support, and maintenance of printers to meet the business requirements.
Network Management 1. Network Capacity Planning 2. Network Topology Documentation 3. Network Load/Impact Analysis 4. Modem Connection Setup and Access 5. New Network Connectivity Mgt 6. Naming Services Conflict Resolution	The deliverables that will be generated out of these services include reliable, available, and serviceable network access and connectivity to business-required data and processing.

5.1.2 Determine the Value and Price of the Product/Service

In the project that stimulated the writing of this book, perceived value, as well as actual value being received, was a key element in the analysis of services and their delivery. The value of the services IT provides is derived from the user's perception and may not have a clear relationship with cost. The determination of the cost of the services is treated in a later section of this chapter. To mix metaphors, the level of value is in the eyes of the beholder or user.

The traditional calculation of value in the business world is return on investment, or ROI. Other more recent measures of value include economic value add, or EVA. The measures of value from this financial or pure business perspective when applied to technology pose significant challenges. Allocating capital investments to specific technology initiatives, as well as identifying and accurately capturing revenue-generated or cost savings directly related to these initiatives, may take significant amounts of accounting and finance resources.

This is not to say investments in technology initiatives should not be expected to create value or have fiscal accountability. Application of simple payback calculations, applying a corporate cost of capital burden on top of initiative costs and other straightforward, easy-to-calculate measures are worthwhile efforts. However, the value created from technology initiatives may not be fully or accurately reflected in these often-sterile numbers.

F. Warren McFarlan, in a recent *CIO Magazine* article, raises and answers a pertinent question relative to value. "How can companies know if technology will add value to their businesses? Technology allows businesses to deliver different kinds of value, but how to tease out that value is the biggest headache. Value is not measured in some abstract sense; it's measured against what other competitive offerings are out in the field. The company may be doing better, but then it's doing better in a different competitive universe. It's hard to know if your investment was really a plus, or if it was just holding things equal."[2]

Generally, the resources required to even attempt to accurately account for value in the traditional ROI sense is not worth the time or money spent. The bottom line on the subject of value is that building credibility by delivering quality services repeatedly will ensure the IT organization is creating enterprise level value.

A different approach is tracking value from the perspective of the receiver of the services/product delivered. A subsequent section of the book deals with success metrics that will identify ways to realistically measure the value from a customer satisfaction standpoint.

---

2. F. Warren McFarlan, "ShopTalk," *CIO Magazine*, February 1, 1999. (Reprinted courtesy of *CIO Magazine*. © 1999 CIO Communications, Inc.)

Pricing of services in an enterprise can take the form of chargebacks at a company, division, department, or workgroup level. The chargeback approach often entails receiving a monthly, quarterly, or annual hit to the budget that is not anticipated, explained, or open to negotiation. In other organizations the amount and timing of the charge is negotiated and agreed upon prior to the fiscal period the charge will be incurred. In this latter case, expectations are managed and the "price" to be paid for services are understood, if not fully controllable.

In progressive organizations that take a more competitive approach to technology services, a menu of services to choose from is offered to the enterprise with prices associated with the service. The process associated with this approach often starts with the development of an application. A determination is made at project initiation as to which services will be required to support the application and what level of support will be most appropriate given the criticality of the business effort being supported with technology. The prices offered for the services in this scenario assume that there are options available to the business unit to obtain their services internally, externally, or not "purchase" the service at all.

In this latter case, being sensitive to the market prices that external service providers can offer is very prudent. The incentive to provide a cost-effective, competitively priced, value-laden service is clearly present.

5.1.3 Establish a Distribution or Delivery Vehicle

Once the services required by the enterprise are identified, a vehicle or channel to provide the services must be determined. Of course the channel selection is interdependent upon the cost, value, and pricing of the services.

Different enterprises may have different alternatives available to them, based on internal and external politics, regulatory constraints, and market competition.

Table 5–3 provides a format to analyze the different alternatives available to provide IT services. The alternatives included continuing an existing outsourcing agreement, establishing a new outsourcing agreement, utilizing corporate IT resources to provide the services, along with creating a division level IT data center.

Assumptions:

- A common set of tools to be used will be required across all alternatives
- New processes/procedures will be developed for all alternatives
- Training on new tools and processes/procedures will be the same for all alternatives

Table 5–3   Charting Options

Alternatives	Services Offered	Rank	Level of Service	Rank	Investment Cost	Rank	Ongoing Cost	Rank	Overall Rank
Current Environment	Services listed in current contract		Level dictated by existing contract						
New Outsourcer Proposal	Service listed above plus new requirements		Level to be negotiated for new proposal						
Corporate Data Center	All services as outlined in section above		Two levels, 7X24 and 5X8, with service level guarantees with users						
Internal Data Center	All services as outlined in section above		Two levels, 7X24 and 5X8, with service level guarantees with users						
Composite Rank									

RANK is a 1 to 4 rating given to the specific key attribute associated with the respective alternative. An overall ranking assumes an equal weighting of each attribute.

By utilizing an objective quantifiable chart the major vehicle to dispense services can be evaluated and a supportable decision made.

5.2 Communicate Early and Often—Who, What, When, Where, How

Communicating the status of existing, planned, and end-of-life IT services early will reduce the probability that rumors and misinformation will stymie successful IT service execution. IT staff, users, and management all share the same dislike for surprises. Repeating the message periodically will reinforce the message itself and ensure that the entire audience has the opportunity to be exposed to its contents.

5.2.1 Who

All IT staffs should have sufficient familiarity with IT services to be able to describe the services, benefits, and deliverables to anyone inquiring about them. They should be especially well versed in their area of expertise and be prepared to present details on those services on demand. IT management should be schooled in all the IT services and be capable of presenting them in business terminology. As described in a later section, help desk staff and account managers join IT management in bearing the primary responsibility for marketing and communicating IT services.

5.2.2 What

The focus of communication should be identifying the services and their attributes. A "menu" of services—their description, deliverables, availability, limitations, price, and method of accessing them—should be the basis of all marketing communications. The descriptions of the services should be devoid of technical jargon and be "businessperson readable." The content of communications on services should not be censored, with two exceptions: Confidential information, such as personnel decisions, should not be communicated for obvious reasons; also, the notification of end-of-life service offerings should be carefully planned and executed so as to limit undue stress.

In addition to the more tactical-oriented communications on services, the IT mission statement, strategic objectives, and linkages to business objectives should be publicized at the appropriate levels.

5.2.3 When

There are two paths that IT services communications take. First is a regularly scheduled communiqué that satisfies expectations for a steady flow of information. The frequency can be weekly, monthly, quarterly, or linked to project milestones timing. Second, any significant event—positive, negative, or neutral that impacts the delivery of IT services—should be communicated quickly. Specific circumstances and organizational culture of a case will determine what is significant, and how much content is required, by case basis.

5.2.4 Where

IT services communications should take place wherever the opportunity presents itself. The site where they occur may be in regular meetings, conferences, or in the hallway. Websites and internal and external publications all provide venues for communicating IT services information.

5.2.5 How

Regularly created and distributed reports, such as status reports, will be the backbone of how communications are effected. Articles specific to timely or focused subjects may be written. Presentations should be created for IT management and staff. "Elevator pitches" should be developed for key staff, such as account managers, to prepare them for delivering a pitch for IT services at any time. In many organizations, T-shirts are a most effective communication and motivational tool.

5.3 Define/Communicate the Metrics Upfront—Quality, Cost, Delivery, Value

Setting expectations upfront in terms of QCDV should be based on specifics as much as practical and be supported by a capability to deliver on the expectations set.

5.3.1 Quality

What are the realistic expectations of quality and the range of quality that can be provided? "The 10 Elements of IT Service Quality," as identified by Gartner's D. Tunick in the September 26, 1996 Report, "Marketing the IS Organization: Questions and Answers,"[3] are:

1. Provide basic service well.
2. Listen to your customers; understand their urgency.
3. Ensure reliability—then ensure it again.
4. Establish a service recovery and relief plan for internal customers.
5. Exceed expectations.
6. Design a service system that works for your organization.
7. Handle requests, projects, problems, and priorities fairly.
8. Reward the staff—both IS and non-IS—for coordinated effort.
9. Use IS staff members as a lightning rod for larger problems.
10. Take care of your IS employees. (Reprinted with permission— August 1999.)

Service level agreements (SLAs) are the most effective way to establish a common understanding of what expectations are and what will be delivered to meet those expectations.

An SLA should be in place before a business application is run in the production data center. It will detail the administrative services, supporting configurations (hardware and software), and supporting prac-

---

3. D. Turick, "Marketing the IS Organization: Questions and Answers," GartnerGroup Research Note, September 26, 1996.

tices necessary to meet the application's business requirements. This agreement will be reviewed as needed, but at least annually, to ensure that it is meeting the application's business SLA requirements. At least once a year, a review process should include a customer satisfaction survey and a user satisfaction survey. Critical path interdependencies between applications will resolve to at least the same level as the application requiring the input data. Table 5–4 lists the key attributes/criteria that must be considered in the development of a service level agreement.

Table 5–4   Charting Criteria in an SLA Agreement

Attributes/ Criteria	Mission Critical (1)	Business Critical (2)	Business Efficiency (3)	User Administered (4)
Critical path interdependencies with other applications	Impacts identified and = 1	Impacts identified and = < 2	Impacts identified and = < 3	Impacts identified and = < 4
Equipment capacity usage	Overall average of 1/2 of available resources	Overall average of 2/3 of available resources	Overall average of 3/4 of available resources	Completed for Operational and users' needs
Administrative support	Dedicated resource(s) and on site at all times	Shared on-site resource	Shared on-site resource	As available
Support procedures	Detailed with specific resource(s)	Detailed with shared resource(s)	Detailed with shared resource(s)	Detailed but done as resource available
Documentation	Completed for Operational and users' needs	Completed for Operational and users' needs	Completed for Operational and users' needs	Completed for Operational needs
Training	Completed for users and support staff before putting into production	Completed for users and support staff before putting into production	At least one on-site support staff trained on operational needs	At least one on-site support staff trained on operational needs
Approved "Move to Production" Plan	Complete testing plan (to include "live" dress rehearsals for one reporting cycle)	Complete testing plan (to include "live" dress rehearsals for one reporting cycle)	Complete testing plan (to include "live" dress rehearsals for one week)	Complete testing plan (to include "live" dress rehearsals for one week)

Table 5–4 Charting Criteria in an SLA Agreement (Continued)

Attributes/ Criteria	Mission Critical (1)	Business Critical (2)	Business Efficiency (3)	User Administered (4)
Hardware	Only proven production HW	Only proven production HW	Can use HW not used in production but has been used by user for > 6 mos.	Can use HW not used in production but has been used by user for > 3 mos.
Software (i.e., OS, DBMS, Utilities, etc.)	Only proven production SW	Only proven production SW	Can use SW not used in production but has been used by user for > 6 mos.	Can use SW not used in production but has been used by user for > 3 mos.
Application access control security	Highest	High	Medium	Medium
Data loss	None	None	No more than one business day's work lost	No more than one business day's work lost
Disaster recovery	Immediate	ASAP	When possible	None
SLA review	As change demands but at least annually	As change demands but at least annually	At least annually	At least annually
SLA reporting	Real-time on production issues and periodic per contract	Real-time on production issues and periodic per contract	Periodic per contract	Periodic per contract
Escalation support	Detailed and crisis team handles	Detailed, crisis team called in when necessary	Detailed	Only essentials documented
Security Audits	Scheduled and unannounced	Scheduled and unannounced	Scheduled and unannounced	Scheduled and unannounced

5.3.2 Cost

Identifying, allocating, and charging for services is a critical element in the overall communication package. Much like the commentary on determining value in an earlier section, the resources applied to identifying, capturing, and allocating cost may take more resource investments than are warranted, especially, if the granularity expected is very fine.

Table 5–5 is an example of a straightforward approach used to identify the staffing component of cost.

Other factors, such as hours of operation ($24 \times 7 \times 365$) and help desk and system response time (level of service) must be taken into consideration when developing the service model. Once the number of hours required is determined for each service, a standard loaded cost-per-resource type can be applied to determine the staffing cost.

Staffing costs can then be added to infrastructure costs such as hardware, software, network, maintenance, and facilities to arrive at a total cost of services.

The cost of services must be identified as early as possible, factored into the pricing equation, and communicated to users. This will ensure that they have the opportunity to commit appropriate funding for the services they require to support their business processes.

5.3.3 Delivery

Users must understand how to receive the services they desire and what level of responsiveness should be expected. A central source to initiate request for services is necessary to ensure that all requests are recorded, responded to by the appropriate service provider, and tracked to completion. In the service model defined in this book, the call center is that central receiver of service requests.

In addition to a physically staffed call center, an on-line capability that allows users to request services via an internal Website can reduce the amount of resource required to staff the call center and provide direct access on-line. The service menu described earlier should describe the availability of the service—whether it is available on a $7 \times 24 \times 365$ basis, or only during business hours five days a week—and how to expect it to be delivered.

Table 5–5 Service and Associated Cost Model

Service	Sched or On Dmnd	Freq (per Yr)	UOM	SA Effort Hrs / UOM	Total SA	OSA Effort Hrs / UOM	Total OSA	DBA Effort Hrs / UOM	Total DBA	Clerk Effort Hrs / UOM	Total Clerk	Ntwk Spec Effort Hrs / UOM	Total Ntwk Spec	Mgr Effort Hrs / UOM	Total Mgr
Server monitoring and corrective action 1.2.1.2	O/D	365	Days	1.5	547.5		0		0		0		0		0
Connectivity from outside servers alive and well															
Disk drive capacity with defined limits															
Network connectivity alive and well															
Paging software active															
No runaway processes															
Memory utilization within defined limits															
Ensure all database active after backup process															
Detect problems or bottlenecks															
Analyze performance compared to capacity															
Provide tier II server level support															
Troubleshoot database problems															
Software Event Monitoring															
System Fault Detection															
Disk Fault Detection															
Print Services 1.2.1.3	O/D	260	Days	2	520		0		0		0		0		0
Troubleshooting in the decentralized environment															
Black box hookups															
Software installation/configuration on new printers															
File server management of print queues															
Provide spooling services (software configuration, re-ordering queues to print more critical jobs first)															
Provide secured printing capability where needed for confidential printing															
Resolve printing problems															

(continued)

Service	Sched or On Dmnd	Freq (per Yr)	UOM	SA Effort Hrs / UOM	Total SA	OSA Effort Hrs / UOM	Total OSA	DBA Effort Hrs / UOM	Total DBA	Clerk Effort Hrs / UOM	Total Clerk	Ntwk Spec Effort Hrs / UOM	Total Ntwk Spec	Mgr Effort Hrs / UOM	Total Mgr
Network Management 1.3.2.3.3	S	260	Days		0		0		0		0	1	260	0	0
Analysis of network impacts based on new adds and changes	O/D	21	Server		0		0		0		0	24	504	0	0
Maintain a network topology drawing															
Manage new installations/connects to network															
Network capacity planning															
Setup and maintain modem connections															
Control the granting and revoking of modem access from outside															
Provide naming services resolution															
Add, remove, update a domain															
Total Effort Hours					1068		0		0		0		764		0

	SA	OSA	DBA	Clerical	Network	Manager
Staff Year	2080	2080	2080	2080	2080	2080
Productivity Rate	0.8	0.8	0.8	0.8	0.8	0.8
Vacation	40	40	40	40	40	40
Training	40	40	40	40	40	40
Sick	16	16	16	16	16	16
Total Availability	1568	1568	1568	1568	1568	1568
Raw Resources Needed	0.513221	0	0	0	0.367308	0.880529
Rounded	1	0	0	0	1	0	2

Other Factors
24 x 7 x 365
Customer Sat
LOS

System Assumptions
32 UNIX Servers
22 NT Servers
11 Novell Servers

The status of the service to be delivered should be communicated to the user promptly and regularly until it has been completed. The status may be in the form of e-mails, voice mails, intranet sites, or phone calls.

5.3.4 Value

Value is measured from the perspective of the user's capability to satisfy their customers needs. Measuring value from a traditional ROI standpoint, as addressed in an earlier section, usually does not generate a positive ROI itself when the effort required to produce it is fully considered.

The perception of the user is the most important factor in determining whether value was created or not. Operational statistics such as uptime, response time, and turnarounds are fine for managing IT, but usually don't reflect whether the user received meaningful value.

Assessing how happy the user is with the services received is a major determinant of perceived value. This assessment can be as simple as an e-mail attachment that has a "smiley face," "frowney face," or "so-so face" to respond to the service received. Or, the assessment may be a multipage professionally engineered survey form sent to random users on a regular basis. In addition to the surveys, one-on-one interviews and analysis of help desk calls can be valuable tools to assess the value users perceive they are receiving from their integrated services that are delivered.

Regularly publishing the responses to the surveys will be a motivating force for the suppliers of the services to continually strive for improvement, acknowledge that users' views of what is valuable is important, and help determine which services are in need of rework or elimination.

▶ 5.4 Understand/Identify and Communicate Risk

Setting appropriate expectations is essential, but also identifying and communicating what happens when something is critical.

An Arthur Andersen survey[4] of CEOs, presidents, board members, and CFOs at more than 150 global companies reveals the need to look more carefully at IT risk:

- One in three senior executives does not have any IT risk management process in place; only half of those who do are confident the processes are strong enough.

- Two out of three executives say their companies do not understand IT-related risks well enough.

- Only 13 percent of executives believe IT strategy is well integrated with business strategy.

- Technology professionals are responsible for the daily management of IT-related risk at 51 percent of the companies.

An element of developing the services that will constitute the portfolio of integrated services to support the enterprise should be an assessment of the risk. The risk associated with the delivery of the individual service and the impact on the overall service portfolio should be considered.

Elements of risk that should be included in the assessment are represented in the Andersen survey described above:

Integrity Risk—This risk encompasses all of the risks associated with the authorization, completeness, and accuracy of transactions as they are entered into, processed, summarized, and reported on by the various application systems deployed by an organization.

Relevance Risk—Relevance risk relates to the usability and timeliness of information that is either created or summarized by an application system. Relevance risk ties directly to the information for decision-making risk, as it is the risk associated with not getting the right data/information to the right person/process/system at the right time to allow the right action to be taken.

---

4. "Managing Business Risks in the Information Age," a study by Arthur Andersen and the Economist Intelligence Unit Ltd. (EIU), 1998.

Access Risk—Access risk focuses on the risk associated with inappropriate access to systems, data, or information. It encompasses the risks of improper segregation of duties, risks associated with the integrity of data and databases, and risks associated with information confidentiality, etc.

Infrastructure Risk—This risk is that the organization does not have an effective information technology infrastructure (hardware, networks, software, people, and processes) to effectively support the current and future needs of the business in an efficient, cost-effective, and well-controlled fashion. These risks are associated with the series of IT processes used to define, develop, maintain, and operate an information processing environment (e.g., computer hardware, networks, etc.) and the associated application systems (e.g., customer service, accounts payable, etc.).[4]

The risk associated with the service delivery should be communicated in conjunction with the negotiation of the service level agreement. If risk is to be reduced, there may be additional costs associated with maintaining the lowest level of risk possible. Redundant servers, highly available storage and dual networks are all components of a risk-mitigating environment.

Once risk has been identified, assessed and managed accordingly, when an event occurs that is outside acceptable parameters, the *problem* must be managed. An effective problem management system should be in place to quickly identify out-of-tolerance situations, initiate corrective action, communicate and track resolution activities, and produce a causal analysis.

How quickly and responsively problems are addressed and resolved, despite the existence of a thorough risk management program, will build significant credibility throughout the enterprise.

▶ 5.5 Explain Roles and Responsibilities

The responsibilities for marketing and communicating IT's services is borne by all the IT staff, but some organizational entities have more critical and specific roles to play.

---

4. "Managing Business Risks in the Information Age," a study by Arthur Andersen and the Economist Intelligence Unit Ltd. (EIU), 1998.

5.5.1 Account Management

The role of the account management function as it relates to marketing and communications is one of primary overseer of the flow of information to the user. The account manager is responsible for ensuring that the user is fully informed about the services available to him or her and coordinates the flow of information back from the user to IT. This is not to say that account management is responsible for being the primary or exclusive conduit of information to the user, especially on a day-to-day operational basis. It is that function's responsibility to provide general oversight of the two-way informational flow and ensure that the overall needs of the user are met.

5.5.2 Help Desk

The marketing and communications role that the help desk plays is basically a reactive one as compared to the proactive approach that account management must utilize. The help desk may be the only assessable resource available to users during off hours or nonoperational hours. The help desk must be prepared to provide accurate, timely responses to user queries. The responsibilities of the help desk are to maintain a current base of knowledge and information so as to provide first-level support to users and make them aware of any immediate or projected events that could impact their operation.

5.5.3 IT Management

IT management's role in marketing and communications is to lubricate the information and communication channels so that IT service information can flow easily throughout the IT organization. It is IT management's responsibility to "fly cover" for his or her subordinates that sometimes have to market and communicate service reductions or other news that may be viewed as less than positive. Ensuring that the key channels of communication (account management and help desk) have access to the information they need to do their jobs is also a prime responsibility of IT management.

5.5.4 Operations Management

Operations management's role is to clearly and completely communicate the needs of the users to the IT organization. They have the responsibility of ensuring that user satisfaction of services received and future needs for services are identified and communicated. Both IT and user management must jointly take ownership to ensure services are marketed and communicated fully.

Taking a Customer Approach

The foundation of the Integrated Service Delivery (ISD) is the service model. This is an organized list of services supplied by the ISD organization. The services are a combination of those your customers need and are willing to pay for (direct services), along with those needed by the ISD organization to provide direct services to your customers (indirect services). For example, a service called "server monitoring" might be a direct service that the customer is willing to pay for. From the customer's standpoint, they are not concerned how you provide this service, so long as their servers are monitored and actions are taken to correct problems when they occur. But in order to provide this service, the ISD organization needs to provide an indirect service such as a "paging system." The paging system service is necessary to alert on-call support personnel of problems that need to be fixed. Both direct and indirect services are included in the service model. The service model is the framework for establishing the resource model and cost model.

The service model will become one of the most important communication tools used within the ISD organization. For customers, it shows all the services your organization provides. It is a discussion tool to determine what services the customer requires. Each customer may not need all the services available from the organization. The service model can be viewed as an "a la carte" type of menu in which the customer can choose those services needed. It also helps determine the delta in services not provided, but requested and/or needed by the customer. As an ISD organization, you can determine to add a new service being requested, or decline the business. But in the end, there will be a clear understanding of those services the ISD organization will provide to each customer.

▶ 6.1 Understanding Your Customers' Requirements

Before you can begin to develop the service model you need to understand who your customers are. When speaking of customers, one of the first visions that come to mind is a person purchasing a product or service from a retail store. Although these are indeed customers, broaden the scope of customers to any person that benefits from a service the ISD organization provides. If you're a database administrator, your customers could range from the developer requesting a new database table to the factory worker who uses the database to track inventories. There are customers that you may never see and meet, but still require you to perform your job to the best of your ability. A customer is a person that will request a service or receive a benefit from a service you provide. Approach the development of the service model from your customer's perspective.

Identify who your customers are. Start by writing down a list of your current customers that you provide services to. Next, add to the list customers that you will be seeking in the future. Setting a vision of the type of customers you want to service within your organization can help determine new customers. You will find yourself referring to this list often during the development of the service model. Once you have determined who your customers are or will be, set up the service model to meet their requirements. Keep the customer as the focal point. Without customers, there is no need to provide services.

▶ 6.2 Developing the Service Model

There are several quality tools and techniques you can use in the development of the service model: benchmarking, brainstorming, interviewing, surveying, and the tree diagram. In our example, the first four tools are used to determine what services should be provided; the last, the tree diagram, is used to systemically map the details of the services into a model. The objective of the service model is to list all the services provided by the ISD organization, both direct and indirect. The services should be at such a level that each service can stand as a separate task.

The following is an example of how a service model is built. The use of the quality tools and techniques will be demonstrated.

One of the best ways to begin development of the service model is by using the quality tool, brainstorming. Brainstorming is a spontaneous generation of ideas; in this case, services. Open thinking should be encouraged. Do not be concerned about judging each service idea generated during the session. Try to keep the focus of the brainstorming session on the customers that will receive these services. Refer to the list of customers generated before the session begins. Record as many possible services that can be thought of. The brainstorming session should continue until a point is reached where participants feel the list is exhausted.

Review the brainstorming list and look for services that have the same meaning and could be consolidated into one service. Look for services that are not within the scope of your customer's requirements. Even more important, ask the question—Are there any services missing that the customer requires? Below is a sampling of services generated from a brainstorming session. This list, brainstorm list 6.2.1, will be used to walk through the development of a service model.

6.2.1 Brainstorm List

- Provide server utilization reports
- Monitor for down databases
- ORASERV process alive and well
- Cost reporting to customers
- Troubleshoot database problems
- Servers are running
- Concurrent managers are running
- Prepare yearly billing statements
- Database listener is running
- Maintain server history information
- Maintain paging system

- Detect server bottlenecks
- Ensure transfer agreements in place
- Monitor for database activity
- Monitor for runaway process
- Memory utilization within defined limits
- Daily reporting of server backup failures
- Disk drive capacity within defined limits
- Network connectivity is available
- Troubleshoot server problems

The next step is to organize the services into a tree diagram. A tree diagram is used to systematically map out increasing levels of detail for related goals, tasks, and in this case, services. The approach used to develop the service model uses a concept from the *Project Management Professional (PMP) Handbook* called work breakdown structure, which pictorially resembles a tree diagram. A work breakdown structure, as defined by the Project Management Institute, follows:

> A deliverable-oriented grouping of project elements which organizes and defines the total scope of the project. Each descending level represents an increasingly detailed definition of a project component. Project components may be products or services.[1]

Each tree branch on the work breakdown structure is called a work package. Work packages contain those services that can be grouped together. Each work package is given a name that best represents the collection of services. Work packages will be important in determining the resource load needed to perform all the tasks within the package. Figure 6–1 is an example of a work breakdown structure.

A numbering system is used to keep the work packages organized. The Project Management Body of Knowledge calls this number system the code of accounts. This allows work packages to be used in different formats than the tree diagram, while still keeping the packages organized. The numbering system is applied to the work breakdown structure after work packages are organized.

---

1. 1996, *Project Management Professional (PMP) Handbook*. "A Guide to the Project Management Body of Knowledge," page 171.

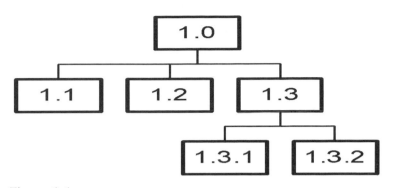

Figure 6–1 Work breakdown structure.

When creating work packages, try to group services by a specific type of skill set. Based on the services generated from the brainstorming session, you should have an idea of what type of skill set is needed. For example, from the brainstorm list 6.2.1, a skill set will be needed to perform server maintenance, database maintenance, and maintain cost/budget control. Knowing that these are the skill sets helps to group the services and name the work packages.

There is no clear-cut or wrong way to group services. The real importance here is being able to identify a group of tasks that can be performed by one skill set. Do not be concerned at this time how many resources will be needed to perform this work package. During the development of the resource model (Chapter 6), you can begin to determine staffing load.

The brainstorm list of services, for example, could be grouped a number of different ways. If you believe all monitoring type activities (database and server) can be performed by the same skill set, then create a work package for monitoring. A second work package could be created for server correction action, and a third for database correction action.

Another approach would be to create a separate work package specifically for server monitoring and correction actions, and a separate work package for database monitoring and correction actions. In this case, you have a skill set experienced in server monitoring and the ability to fix the problems associated with the monitoring routines. A final consideration is that work packages are ever-changing. You will be adjusting, adding, and deleting work packages as the requirements of your customer change.

6.2.2 Work Package Grouping Example List

Server Monitoring and Corrective Action

- Maintain paging system
- Detect server bottlenecks
- Monitor for runaway process
- Servers are running
- Memory utilization within defined limits
- Disk drive capacity within defined limits
- Network connectivity is available
- Troubleshoot server problems

Operations Metrics/Utilizing Reporting

- Provide server utilization reports
- Daily reporting of server backup failures
- Maintain server history information
- Compile server and database statistics

Cost Management

- Ensure transfer agreements are in place
- Cost reporting to customers
- Prepare yearly billing statements
- Maintain charge back model

Database Monitoring and Corrective Action

- Monitoring for down databases
- ORASERV process alive and well
- Monitor for database activity
- Troubleshoot database problems
- Database listener is running

Once work packages are created, they are then grouped into a tree diagram, known as the service Model. Figure 6–2 shows how the work packages from list 6.2.2 form a service model. Notice additional title boxes were created to group individual work packages. Title boxes are used only for grouping work packages. There are no services directly related to a title box. From list 6.2.2, title box Monitor 1.2.1 was created to group Server Monitoring and Corrective Action 1.2.1.1 and Database Monitoring and Corrective Action 1.2.1.2. A Support Services 1.2 title box was created to group Monitor 1.2.1 and Operations Metrics/Utilization Reporting 1.2.2. Finally, Integrated Service Delivery 1.0 was created to group all work packages under one package.

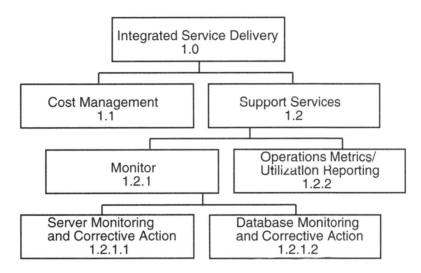

Figure 6–2 Creating title boxes from work packages.

Once you have completed the brainstorming session and organized the results into a service model tree diagram, there are several alternatives on how to proceed. One is to hold another brainstorming session to see if the team can generate more services. Adding and/or changing some team members might help to get new thinking in the session and uncover missing services. Start off this second brainstorming session by reviewing the service model tree diagram. Using self-stick pieces of paper to generate new ideas will allow for easy placement of the services into the service model tree diagram.

Another alternative is to proceed by using one of the other quality tools—benchmarking, interviewing, and surveying. These tools can be used in any order or simultaneously, especially when there are time lapses in completion of the activities.

Benchmarking can be used to learn about the services provided by other competitors or those companies recognized as leaders in their field as information technology service providers. Benchmarking is a way to identify services that are common across all IT service providers. It should be used as a means to validate the ISD service model with other competitors. It can also be used to continuously redefine the service model to keep a competitive advantage in the marketplace.

Interviewing and/or surveying involves getting the input from the customers. Since the service model is being built around the needs and wants of the customer, it is essential that at least one of these forms of customer involvement activities takes place. Interviewing can be done with individual customers or groups of customers. Although interviewing can be done over the phone, an in-person interview allows facial expressions of the customer to be seen and judged.

Surveying is a type of interviewing done on paper via a questionnaire. Surveying takes considerably more time. First, a survey has to be generated—this alone is no small task. The survey needs to be distributed to the customers. The customer has to respond to the survey and return it to you. Finally, the results of the survey have to be analyzed. The elapsed time could be months before useful information is obtained. It is recommended that you only use surveying when your customers are not available for face-to-face interviews or phone interviews. Phone interviews might not be an option to global customers due to the different time zones. There also might be a language barrier that could be overcome by the written communication of a survey.

With interviewing or surveying the objective is to gain customer buy-in to the service model. This is accomplished by reviewing the service model and seeking out those services that are missing and/or not needed. This also gives the customer a sense of being part of the building process.

▶ 6.3   One-Stop Shopping—Seamless Delivery

The service model should provide one-stop shopping for customers looking for IT services. The service model used at Xerox Corporation to provide support to the manufacturing and distribution operations contained five major work packages: Program Management 1.1, Support Services 1.2, Operations 1.3, Asset Planning and Control 1.4, and Help Desk 1.5. The service model was created with input and buy-in from the customers. The quality tools brainstorming, benchmarking, interviewing, and surveying were all used in the development process of the service model. Each of the five major work packages will be reviewed here.

6.3.1 Project Management

Program Management 1.1 contains many of the services necessary for support of the ISD organization. This is where many of the indirect services are located. One of the most important services in management of organization is contained in the Program Management work package. This is the level of service (LOS) agreement between the service provider and the customer. Because of this, there are a number of services placed in the service model to ensure that the LOS created is agreed to and maintained. Customer review sessions and service level improvement planning are two of the services that continue the process of customer involvement and support the LOS agreement.

This branch of the service model also deals with cost management. The cost charge-back model is maintained within this area. This includes the renewal of transfer agreements between organizations, and cost reporting to the customer and management to keep people informed of the current cost status.

In developing the service model at Xerox Corporation, one of the services the customers requested was project management. The customer was interested in being able to turn to one service provider when needing a resource to lead a project through its life cycle. A specific work package was created to provide services to support project management such as requirements gathering and project coordination. Figure 6–3 shows the services of the Program Management work package.

- LOS Management 1.1.1
  — Services Documentation and Publication
  — Service Requirements Gathering
  — Service Level Agreement Development
  — Service Level Execution Coordination
  — Service Level Monitoring and Reporting
  — Service Level Improvement Planning

- Cost Management 1.1.2
  — Service Cost Determination
  — Cost Chargeback Model Maintenance
  — Cost Transfer Establishment and Agreement
  — Cost Reporting
  — Cost Improvement

- Project Management 1.1.3
  — Requirements Gathering and Documentation
  — Service Delivery Coordination
  — Customer Engagement Management

Figure 6–3   Program Management work package.

6.3.2   Support Services

The Support Services 1.2 work package (Figure 6–3) was created to group services centered on system monitoring, and tuning and maintenance of servers and databases. Reporting metrics on utilization of the environment and users support requests such as password resets, are included. The thinking here was to group ongoing type service activities that ensure continual operations of the environment. The three services in this work package could be performed by junior- and intermediate-level skill-set people with the proper processes and procedures in place. This would free the senior level people to concentrate on new development projects and be called in only when problems have escalated.

- Monitoring 1.2.1
  - Performance Tuning 1.2.1.1
    - Performance Problems Analysis and Support
    - Server, Net, and DB Performance Statistic Analysis
    - Server, Net, and DB Performance Tuning
  - Server Monitoring and Corrective Action 1.2.1.2
    - Tier II Level Support
    - Internal and External Connectivity Monitoring
    - DB Activity Monitoring
    - Capacity/Utilization/Performance Monitoring
    - Process Execution Monitoring
    - Day of Operations Troubleshooting
    - Day of Operations Problem Resolution
  - Print Services 1.2.1.3
    - Hardware/Software Installation and Configuration
    - Print Queue and Spooling Management
    - Secured Printing Management
    - Printing Problem Troubleshooting and Resolution
  - Ongoing DB Monitoring and Maintenance 1.2.1.4
    - Database Activity Monitoring
    - ORASRV Process Monitoring
    - DB Manager Activity Monitoring

- Reporting 1.2.2
  - Operations Metrics/Utilization Reporting 1.2.2.1
    - Daily Operations Activities Reporting
    - Shift Turnover Reporting
    - Server, DB, and Net Statistic Compilation
    - Operations Statistics History Maintenance
    - Operations Statistics Reporting

- User Services 1.2.3
  - Application Server Support 1.2.3.1
    - Application Software Consulting
    - Application Software Installation Assistance
    - Application Tuning
    - Directories Setup
    - Job Setup, Scheduling, and Monitoring
  - Application Database Support 1.2.3.2
    - Application Database Consulting
    - SQL Code Analysis
    - Testing and Evaluation Assistance
  - Engineering Support 1.2.3.3
    - New Technology Research, Testing, and Installation
    - Benchmark Lab Support
    - Interoperability of New Hardware Software Testing

Figure 6–4 Support Services work package.

6.3.3 Operations

The Operations 1.3 work package outlined in Figure 6–4 contains the largest number of services. This work package contains three main work packages. The first is the server work package, which concentrates on the tasks for the server environments. This includes services such as backup and recovery, new server installations, and server documentation. In this work package we identify three levels of skills sets: senior, immediate, and junior.

The second work package centers on software. Services such as software installations, distributions of software to other servers, change control functions, and job scheduling are grouped in this area. One of the requirements from our customers was internal distribution of software to other manufacturing sites around the world. Services such as software configuration, release scheduling, and media creation were added to support the customer's requirement.

- Server 1.3.1
  - Server Backup/Recovery 1.3.1.1
    - Backup Schedule Creation and Maintenance
    - Daily, Weekly, and Monthly Backup Execution
    - Backup Monitoring, Troubleshooting, and Reporting
    - Media Storage, Retention, and Retrieval
  - Server Installation/Setup 1.3.1.2
    - Standard Server Configuration Utilization
    - Facilities Coordination
    - Hardware and Software Installation
    - Hardware and Software Setup and Configuration
    - Monitoring, Alerting, and Reporting Established
  - Server Documentation 1.3.1.3
    - Standard Server Configuration Maintenance
    - Server Run Book Documentation and Maintenance
    - Operations Processes Documentation
  - Client "New" Application Install/Deinstallation 1.3.1.4
    - Client Software Installation
    - Client Network Connection Setup and Configuration
    - Client Workstation Connectivity Testing
    - Client Access Troubleshooting
  - Server Security 1.3.1.5
    - Server Security Procedures Documentation
    - Server Access Security Maintenance
    - Print Security Oversight

Figure 6–5 Operations work package.

- Software 1.3.2
  - Installation 1.3.2.1
    - Server Software Installation 1.3.2.1.1
      - Operating System Installation
      - Tools Installation
      - Vendor Utilities Installation
      - Software Upgrade Maintenance
    - Oracle Software 1.3.2.1.2
      - Test Plan Creation
      - Oracle Parameter/Settings Setup
      - Database Related Installation
      - Directory Structure Setup and Review
      - RDBMS Test Plan Execution
      - User Connectivity Support
      - Software Patch Management
  - Distribution 1.3.2.2
    - Release Scheduling/Packaging 1.3.2.2.1
      - Release Scheduling Creation and Management
      - Software Release Content Definition
      - Release Related Script Development
      - Release Preparation
      - Release Documentation Preparation
      - Release and Script Testing
    - Software Distribution 1.3.2.2.2
      - Media Creation
      - Media Unloading Testing
      - Media Unloading Documentation
      - Target Site Requirements Documentation
      - Release Move to Production
      - Release Assistance and Consulting
  - Control 1.3.2.3
    - Change Control 1.3.2.3.1
      - Events Under Change Control Definition
      - Change Event Recordation
      - Change Notification
      - Change Tracking and Reporting
      - Change Analysis/Prioritization
      - Change Approval Coordination
      - Change Closeout
    - Vendor Software Version Control 1.3.2.3.2
      - S/W, Configuration, and Version Inventory
      - Licensing Agreement Management

Figure 6–5 Operations work package. (Continued)

- Network Management 1.3.2.3.3
  — Network Capacity Planning
  — Network Topology Documentation
  — Network Load/Impact Analysis
  — Modem Connection Setup and Access
  — New Network Connectivity Management
  — Naming Services Conflict Resolution
— Application 1.3.2.4
  - Oracle Application Management 1.3.2.4.1
    — Tier II Support
    — Troubleshoot Application Problems
    — Printer Registration and Configuration
    — Application Security Model Definition
    — Software Customization Support
  - Job Scheduling/Execution 1.3.2.4.2
    — Operational Plan Publishing
    — Application Job Schedule Setup and Maintenance
    — Concurrent Manager Setup
    — Job Execution Management
    — Job/Task DB Maintenance
    — Execution Troubleshooting

- DBA 1.3.3
  — Database Administration 1.3.3.1
    - Tier II Level Support
    - Database Capacity Planning
    - Database Sizing and Creation
    - Physical Data Model Implementation
    - Database Tuning
    - Database Backup, Retrieval and Restoring
    - Database Problem Troubleshooting
  — Database Security 1.3.3.2
    - Database Security Schema Setup
    - Database Password Management
    - Audit Trail Management
    - Database Access Granting and Revoking
    - Database Access Review and Reporting

Figure 6–5 Operations work package. (Continued)

The third work package contains services associated with database administration. In this work package many of the normal database administration functions such as database sizing, creation, and tuning can be found. The skill set to support this work package is the senior to immediate range. Tasks such as database password resets, database monitoring, and database reports are found in the support service help desk work packages, which are supported by junior level skill sets.

6.3.4 Asset Planning and Control

Asset Planning and Control is another set of key services important to keep the organization running. The mind-set here was to centralize the asset planning, purchasing, and control into one organization that would have the responsibility to focus on asset management. Before centralization of these services, many customers performed their own procurement of materials and developed one-off systems to track the assets. There was little synergy between customers. Each customer had their own processes to support these activities.

For example, procurement was another service requested by the customers during our interviewing sessions. Customers often complained about how painful the procurement process was. By offering it as a service, one group could become proficient in the procurement process.

Even though many customers did have a one-off tracking system for assets, they did not pay enough attention to it. Maintenance on assets would often expire, only to be uncovered when a service call was needed and rejected by the vendor. Customers would also struggle to keep an updated list of all the assets, and their location and lease expiration dates. At times, because lease expiration dates on assets would go unnoticed, penalties would occur. Because of these issues, asset tracking was offered as a service. Figure 6–6 shows the elements of the Asset Planning and Control work package.

6.3.5 Help Desk

The Help Desk 1.5 work package (Figure 6–7) contains services to support a help desk call center, problem management, and training support. Xerox Corporation wanted the help desk to be more than just call routing. Our objective in creating this work package was to move services into this area that would allow the help desk personnel to gain experience that would enable them to grow into other jobs.

- Procurement 1.4.1
  - Server Procurement 1.4.1.1
    - Customer Needs Definition Assistance
    - Hardware Compatibility Validation
    - Hardware/Equipment Purchasing

- Asset Management 1.4.2
  - Asset/Configuration Management 1.4.2.1
    - Equipment Labeling and Documenting
    - Serial #, Location, and Owner Tracking
    - Lease Management
  - Maintenance Agreements (SW & HW) 1.4.2.2
    - Level of Maintenance Determination
    - Vendor Service Coordination
    - Service Scheduling Coordination
  - Server/HW Capacity Planning 1.4.2.3
    - Server and Related Equipment Utilization Tracking
    - Growth Trend Analysis and Projection
    - Annual Capacity Planning Reporting
    - Customer Capacity Threshold Reporting

- Facilities 1.4.3
  - Disaster Recovery Planning
  - Computer Room Space Planning
  - Computer Room Environmental Planning
  - Physical Security Management
  - Ongoing Security Audit Coordination
  - Security Breach Investigation and Reporting
  - Overall Security Monitoring

Figure 6–6   Asset Planning and Control work package.

To support this objective, one of the services that was placed within the Help Desk work package was the user profile management. This involved the creation of user accounts, password resets, printer setup—the type of activities that might be placed in the Operations work package. This enables the help desk to provide tier 1 and tier 2 support, along with providing valuable work experience to the help desk personnel.

Training was another group of services placed into the Help Desk work package. The idea here was to get the help desk personnel to provide training to the customers. The help desk personnel would be able to meet the customers and put a face to the name of the person placing a help desk call. It also gives the Help Desk an understanding of the type of problems and concerns customers are facing with their applications.

- Training 1.5.1
  — New User Startup Training Coordination
  — Workstation Training Coordination
  — Training Material Validation
  — Classroom Training Support

- Call Center 1.5.2
  — Service Request Management 1.5.2.1
    - Service Request Recording, Routing, and Tracking
    - Service Metrics and Utilization Reporting
    - On-call and Contact List Maintenance and Publishing
    - Escalation Procedure Maintenance
    - Service Request Monitoring and Analysis
  — User Profile Management 1.5.2.2
    - New Account Creation
    - Account Deletion
    - Account Security Setup
    - Password Assignment
    - Unix Grouping Assignment
    - Application Menu and Responsibilities Setup
    - User Account Records Maintenance

- Software Problem Management/Patch Process 1.5.3
  — Problem Recording, Tracking, and Reporting
  — Problem Analysis and Solution Determination
  — Problem Resolution and Closure
  — Vendor SW Problem Tracking and Reporting
  — Software Patch Testing and Installation

Figure 6–7 Help Desk work package.

Figure 6–8 is a tree diagram used to systematically map out the services described in the previous sections. Each work package can be mapped back to the services outlined by using the "code of account" number. For example, "Support Service 1.2" maps back to section 6.3.2 Support Services. The tree diagram is just one example of how to display offered services to the customer.

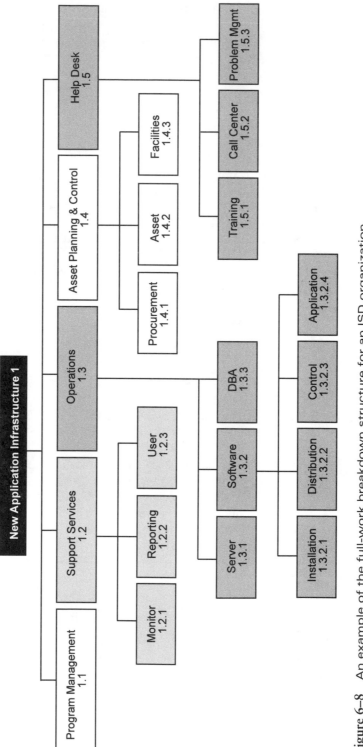

Figure 6–8   An example of the full-work breakdown structure for an ISD organization.

Chapter **6** | Taking a Customer Approach

6.4 Customer Satisfaction

We define customer satisfaction as a measurement of how well the organization is performing from the customer's perspective. Having defined an agreed upon level of service for each customer gives them a clear understanding on which to base their satisfaction with the ISD organization. Not having this clear understanding, customers could be basing their satisfaction on a service not even provided. For example, "Office Printer Support" might not be a service provided by the ISD organization, but provided by another organization or maybe provided internally by the customers themselves. The office printer might need to have the ink drum changed. The customer places a call to the help desk and requests this service. Instead of the help desk just rejecting the customer on this request, they can now refer to the service model and inform the customer that this is a service not provided per the agreed service model and LOS.

The service model provides a framework for the development of metrics, against which the organization is rated. This documents a clear understanding for both the customer and supplier of expectation levels in key areas. The metrics not only spell out expectations of the supplier, but those of the customer as well. For example, "Skills Achievement" of the employees using the applications can be a metrics to judge the knowledge level of the employees (customers) using the applications. This could be rated against a certification test that each employee must take. Ensuring that the employees are trained and understand the applications they are working in will increase the customer satisfaction level.

When the service model is taken to the next step, a tier support level document is developed that shows not only what services are provided by the organization, but also outlines all the services required by the customers and shows the service provider for each service.

Processes and Procedures

▶ 7.1 Introduction

Processes and procedures provide the framework for a quality organization. Tasks that are performed on a routine basis should be developed into a procedure. Every staff team member should use these procedures and continually enhance them as needed. They are especially important for new team members to ensure that they follow the standards developed by the ISD organization. Processes and procedures also enable the ISD organization to become predictable. Customers will become accustomed to and accept certain things from the ISD organization. For example, the customer will recognize how problems are communicated to them in the same fashion each time and in the same format. This will help improve customer satisfaction.

▶ 7.2 Customer Communication

Customer communication processes and procedures focus on delivering timely information to the customer. Most discussions on poor customer satisfaction usually lead back to a lack of communication. Customers hate not knowing what is happening in their environment.

We could all probably relate to an experience where some event took place that we had little or no control over. This created frustration and dissatisfaction on our part. It could be as simple as waiting in a checkout line at the supermarket in which the line wasn't moving. Your anxiety grows as you witness the cashier and the customer ahead of you just standing around, seemly waiting for something, and thinking to yourself, should I move to a new line or should I wait it out? You become frustrated, not because you have to wait, but because you do not know what the problem is and how long it might be before it is resolved. If the cashier was able to take a moment and communicate to you why there was a holdup, you would gain that "sense of control" we all seek. Frustration would begin to diminish and you would now be able to make a decision about moving to a new line or waiting it out.

Customers of IT organizations sense that same level of frustration and dissatisfaction when problems occur with their computing environment that they are not informed of. It might not be possible to let each customer know personally what the problems are, but there are several customer communication processes that can be implemented to improve overall communications. These processes are:

- Help Desk Notification
- Customer Escalation
- Customer Contact List
- Exception Reporting
- Schedule Outage Notification

By implementing these customer communication processes, you are one step closer to improving customer satisfaction. However, to fully implement these processes, each one must be reviewed with the customer and, most importantly—get customer buy-in!

In the ISD organization, the enforcement of team members adhering to the processes and procedures is the responsibility of the ISD management team. The management team must ensure that every person on his or her team understands and follows the processes. One way to ensure processes are followed is to make them part of the employee's performance review. Set goals that key processes in the organization are followed 100 percent of the time. Then review the goals quarterly to reinforce the importance of following processes.

Other methods to enforce the importance of adhering to processes are: post key processes in the office area of employees; have the processes enlarged into poster size; or reduce the processes to credit card size to be carried by employees in their wallet.

7.2.1 Help Desk Notification Procedure

Because of extensive proactive monitoring, the ISD team usually recognizes problems before the customer realizes the same problems. By putting in place an internal help desk notification procedure, the ISD organization is able to communicate the problem to the customer in a timely fashion. Below is an example of an internal ISD help desk notification procedure where an ISD team member (SA, DBA, OSA) notifies the help desk of the problem. The help desk then communicates the problem to the customers. It also prepares the help desk for calls that might be coming in related to the problem.

7.2.1.1 Help Desk Notification

When an infrastructure-related problem occurs, the ISD team (SAs, DBAs, OSAs, etc.) will call the help desk as soon as possible to notify them of the problem. Because of extensive proactive monitoring, the ISD team recognizes problems before the customer is aware of the same problem. The help desk will then call "key" customers and inform them of the problem and probable resolution time. This also gives the help desk advance notice of any new calls that might be received because of the problem. The help desk is then able to properly communicate the problem and estimated resolution time. At the conclusion (resolution) of the problem the ISD team will contact the help desk and request the "key" customer be contacted with the new status. For priority 1 problems, the ISD team will call the help desk every two hours or an agreed upon time frame to update the status of the problem.

There are times when the customer bypasses the help desk and calls the ISD team member directly about a problem with their computing environment. When this occurs, the ISD team member should inform the customer to call the help desk to open a ticket. Even though the ISD team member asked the customer to call the help desk, the ISD team member also needs to call the help desk to inform them of the problem and the estimated resolution time. The customer is responsible for opening the ticket. The ISD team member is responsible for updating the ticket with the current status.

Examples of events in which the help desk should be notified:

- Scheduled maintenance shutdown (planned with customers)
- Scheduled shutdown for hardware replacement (medium urgency)
- Emergency shutdowns
- Downed databases and servers
- Known problems including slowdowns and technical outages

The help desk will open a ticket when a customer has called to report an issue or problem and close the ticket when the ISD team member calls to state the issue has been resolved. The ISD team member is responsible for follow-up written communication on the problem per the exception report process.

7.2.2 Customer Escalation Process

There are certain computing environment problems that require the ISD team to disrupt customers by taking some action to fix the problem. This usually involves bouncing a database, rebooting a server, or taking a server down for an extended period of time to fix a hardware problem. When action is required to fix a problem that will affect the system availability, the customer escalation process needs to be followed. This process gets the customer involved in making the decision. Since the action to fix the problem usually occurs outside the window of allowable system downtime, it is important to get customer buy-in to the action being taken.

An ISD team member initiates this process when he recognizes a system problem that needs attention. The process outlines exactly which customers are the decision makers in the organization. These are the customers that need to be called to get buy-in to the recommended action to be taken. The customer and the ISD team member jointly make a decision on how to resolve the problem. Below is an example of this process.

7.2.2.1 Customer Escalation

The escalation process needs to be followed when a condition occurs with a server and/or database that is outside the LOS agreement. Most production servers have an LOS agreement that requires the server and database to be available seven days a week, 22 hours a day. The operations schedule shows the LOS uptime requirement for each server. The following examples are conditions that follow the escalation process:

- When a server/database needs to be taken down during the LOS uptime, the customer should be informed of the condition and given the options available to correct the problem. The customer has the option to wait until the scheduled downtime to fix the condition.

- When a server/database has come down on its own, the customer should be informed of the condition and the plan for resolution.

Some examples of occurrences that causes escalation conditions:

- Hardware failure and replacement during LOS uptime
- Server hang and reboot during LOS uptime
- Database shutdown and startup to clear locks during LOS uptime

Use the customer contact list to identify who needs to be contacted in the customer escalation process. The customer contacts are bolded, the technical contacts are in italics, and the managerial contacts are printed in normal font.

When a condition occurs that needs to be escalated:

- Call the primary customer contacts. If they are not available, leave a message about the condition and inform them of the actions you will be taking.
- Call the ISD team leaders.
- Call the ISD help desk to inform them of the condition and plan for resolution.

7.2.2.2 *Customer Contact List*

One of the keys to effective customer communication is knowing who your customers are and how to reach them. The customer contact list provides the ISD team with technical contacts as well as customer contacts. Table 7–1 shows an example of a customer contact list. It lists the customer by server and the application that the customer is associated with. The list is used for several customer communication processes and procedures.

Table 7–1 The Customer Contact List

Server	Application	Customer Notification
UNIX-12 UNX1-3 NT-01	ERP	**Nino Thomas 555-1212** **Anthony Jones 555-1212** Sally Figure Jane Smith ISD Manager – Joe Good Help Desk 555-1212 SA Team DL
UNIX-A1	Multi National Purchasing (MNP)	**Mary Worker – 555-4435** ISD Manager – Joe Good Help Desk 555-1212 SA Team DL
WEB-01 CAL-01 ATL-05		**Maura Reilly 555-1211** **Jay Hughes 555-1212** **Maria Tardugno 555-1181** Deb King Tom Connie Mark Banks ISD Manager – Joe Good Help Desk 555-1212
UNIX-76 NT-12	HR	**Steven Jones 555-1212** **Albert Tomm 555-1212** **Catherine Tardugno 555-9110** ISD Manager – Joe Good Help Desk 555-1212 SA Team DL

Chapter **7** | Processes and Procedures

Not only is it important to communicate with the customer, it is also important to keep key members of the ISD organization informed. In the example below we have chosen to add the help desk, SA manager, DBA manager, and operations manager to the list in addition to the customer. It is the responsibility of the managers to forward to their team as needed.

Table 7–1 outlines the contact points to be used for escalation, exception, and schedule outage communications. The person(s) in bold are used for escalation processes in which phone calls are made. They are also to be included with the rest of the people in written communication for exception and schedule outage.

7.2.3 Exception Reporting Process

Exception reporting is a formal written notification to the customer informing them of a problem with their computing environment. The exception report is usually after the fact. It has a set format and must be delivered within 24 hours of the problem to provide timely information to the customer. It is the ISD team leader's responsibility to complete and send out the exception report. The customer contact list is used to determine the distribution of the report.

7.2.3.1 Exception Reporting

Customers will be notified via e-mail within 24 hours of a server exception condition. Use Table 7–1 to find the customer notification list based on the server and application that experienced the exception. Be aware that some servers have multiple applications. If the exception is serverwide, send the notification to all application customers on the server.

Server exception notices must be sent under the following conditions:

- Failed production gzips (database backups)
- Failed refreshes of production DSS databases
- Server down outside of LOS agreement
- Equipment failure
- Network outage

- Server down
- User connectivity failure due to server-related issue

Exception Report Format

DATE —date and time of exception condition.

PROBLEM DEFINITION—what server, database software, etc., had the condition, along with a short description of the problem?

ROOT CAUSE—what caused the problem?

RESOLUTION—how the problem was fixed.

FOLLOW-UP ACTIONS—what will be done in the future to prevent the problem from reoccuring?

Exception Report Example

DATE—2/23/96, 6 A.M.

PROBLEM DEFINITION—Production server UNIX-03 not restoring database correctly.

ROOT CAUSE

1. It was found that the scripts were not working correctly due to a permission problem in the ORACLE and ORAAPPS accounts.
2. The ".rhosts" files in the ORACLE and ORAAPPS home directories were rearranged, with root having the least permissions for equivalency.

RESOLUTION—Both ".rhosts" files were corrected and the refresh, gzips, and database start/stops were tested manually. All scripts were tested and verified to work correctly.

FOLLOW-UP ACTIONS—A follow-up note explaining the importance of the file will be distributed.

▶ 7.3 Internal Communication Processes and Procedures

The first section of this chapter we discussed processes that dealt with keeping the customer informed. Just as important as keeping the customer informed is keeping the ISD team informed. Internal communication processes and procedures are needed to ensure that the ISD team operates as a cohesive unit. Processes that aid in this effort are:

- Help Desk Off-Hour Escalation
- Team Contact List
- Vendor Contact List
- ISD Internal Request Procedure
- Change Control Process

7.3.1 Help Desk Off-Hour Escalation Process

Most organizations don't have the luxury of keeping skilled technical staff on-site seven days a week, 24 hours a day. Instead, they rely on some type of on-call process to provide technical support to their customers during off-hours. The help desk is usually the source responsible for contacting the technical resources when needed. To enable the help desk to perform this task, an on-call list is maintained showing the technical resources on call and how to reach them. But what happens when the person on call is not responding to the help desk call/page? The customer is expecting a return call from the ISD organization based on the LOS agreement. To ensure customer satisfaction, the ISD organization needs to have an internal escalation procedure in place that would enable the help desk to find a technical resource.

Figure 7–1 lists an internal help desk call process for reaching on-call personnel during off-hours. The assumption being that during normal work hours (Monday–Friday, 8 A.M.–5 P.M.) the resources should be on-site and be able to respond within an acceptable time period. It is also based on the assumption that the customer's LOS states a two and one half-hour (2½) call back for a technical support person. If the call-back period needs to be shorter, adjust the times in the escalation process as required.

7.3.1.1 Help Desk Off-Hour Escalation

The help desk calls or pages the primary person on-call at, say, 8 P.M. This is the start of the "elapsed time" column showing "0:00." When the elapsed time reaches 15 minutes (clock time 8:15 P.M.), the help desk then calls or pages the primary person again for the second time.

The help desk then waits till one and one half hours have gone by (clock time 9:30 P.M.) before then calling or paging the primary person and secondary person on-call. When you follow the call sequence to the bottom, the last call is to the ISD Manager two hours and forty-five minutes after (clock time 10:45 P.M.) the first call/page was placed.

Elapsed Time in Minutes	Help Desk Action
0:00	Help Desk pages primary on-call person
0:15	Help Desk pages primary on-call person for the second time
1:30	Help Desk pages primary on-call for third time. Help Desk pages secondary on-call for first time
1:45	Help Desk calls home phone number of primary on-call
1:46	Help Desk pages primary on-call for fourth time
1:47	Help Desk pages secondary on-call second time
2:00	Help Desk calls home phone number of secondary on-call
2:01	Help Desk pages secondary on-call for third time
2:15	Help Desk calls home phone of Team Leader
2:16	Help Desk pages Team Leader
2:30	Help Desk calls home phone of Technical Manager
2:31	Help Desk pages Technical Manager
2:45	Help Desk calls home phone of ISD Manager
2:46	Help Desk pages ISD Manager

Figure 7–1   Help desk call process.

7.3.2   Team Member and Vendor Contact Lists

Along with an internal help desk escalation process, there should be several documents in place to assist the ISD team members. Two of the more important documents are: (1) a team member list, and (2) vendor contact information. These might seem like very routine documents that any IS organization would maintain, but in many IT organizations they are nonexistent. The format of the documents is not important, so long as the key information is present.

These documents come in handy during off-hours system problems when the ISD staff is usually at home and needs help with a problem. These documents enable the on-call person to contact other team members and/or vendors to assist them in the problem. The last thing you want to be doing while working on a system problem is searching for phone numbers to get help.

Team Member List

	Work	Home	Pager
Database Administrators			
JJ Hughes	555-1212	444-1234	340-1234
Maura Tomm	555-3214	543-1398	340-6552
Joe Tardugno	555-2311	543-1438	340-6421
UNIX System Administrators			
Rachael Hughes	555-5421	444-9502	340-5421
Grace Dunnigan	555-3551	235-4421	340-5541
Albie DiPasquale	555-2134	349-0092	340-9985
Novell/NT System Administrators			
Nino DiPasquale	555-2351	321-3313	340-1230
Nicholas Tardugno	555-0613	321-2931	340-2310
Stephen Hughes	555-0694	321-0098	340-9981

Vendor Contact List

Computer Center Modems	
East Corner, bldg. 431	543-1515
West Corner, bldg. 431	542-1515
Paging System Modem	541-1515
Backup Modem	540-1515

```
Sun Microsystems              1-800-872-4786

    Contract # SC123456

    Escalation Manager        555-1212


Baydel Corporation            1-800-4BAYDEL

    Customer Support No.      1998877

    Escalation Manager        1-888-1234


Oracle Corporation            1-800-555-1212

    CSI # 123435

    GOLD Support Manager      406-554-3099


Citrix Software Support

    1-800-424-8749            M-F, 8A.M.-9P.M.

    1-800-555-1212            all other times
```

7.3.3   ISD Internal Request Procedure

The ISD organization supports customers within its own organizations (DBA, OSA, developers) and customers outside the organization. A process needs to exist to manage the daily incoming requests for simple tasks. There is no need to open up formal projects for simple requests such as directory creations, account creations, special backups, and file restores. A request process should be defined to allow customers to submit simple requests into the ISD organization. Below is an example of a request process.

7.3.3.1 ISD Internal Request Process

This procedure is to be followed to request standard UNIX and NT tasks such as: creation of directories and automount points, addition/ changes to backup schedules, load tapes, special tape creation, changes to file and directory privileges, and running a script that requires root privileges. These standard tasks, in general, should not take more than one hour to complete, and are completed between Monday and Friday, 8 A.M. to 5 P.M.

For tasks that consume more than an hour, require a special element, and/or require special timing, it is best to request that the task be put on a project schedule and assigned a systems administrator.

Account creation and password-reset requests are handled by calling the help desk. For new accounts, an account form needs to be created (see the following steps).

1. E-mail a message to requests@yourcompany.com with the word "request:" in the subject line.*

2. A UNIX or NT SA will respond by e-mail within 24 hours after they received the request. Within the e-mail they will state the approximate completion time of the request. For requests that can be completed within 24 hours, just a completion notification is sent.

3. If *no* response is received from the SA team within 24 hours, the person making the request can escalate the request to the systems manager either by VMAX or e-mail. The systems manager will follow up with a phone message and e-mail to the person making the request.

4. If there is no response to the request within 48 hours, the person making the request should contact the technical operations manager.

5. A UNIX administrator will communicate via e-mail when the request has been completed.

---

* For emergency requests, clearly identify "emergency request:" in the subject line. These are requests that are standard in scope, but need to be accomplished within a short time frame.

▶ 7.4 Change Control Process

Every ISD organization needs a change control process. Change control can be a very complex process, consisting of a formal review process, weekly change meetings, and several levels of approval processes. It can also be a simple tracking process that is completed after the change has taken place. Most organizations probably use some combination of the two. Below is a sample change control process.

7.4.1 Change Control

Establish a process to manage and track system change requests within the IT group, especially changes to the application servers and applications themselves. All system change requests are to be submitted to the help desk, which will function as both the control point and tracking point for all changes.

- Complete the system change request with all related information explaining problem statement, details of change, backup requirements, testing process, implementation impacts, and execution date.
- Submit new system change requests directly to the help desk.
- The help desk will assign a number to the system change request and enter this into the change request tracking database.
- The help desk will distribute the change control request to the affected customers. This will serve as notification of the change.
- The help desk will generate periodic reports of all system change requests to the list activity.
- Change notification request periods are based on the type of change:
  1) Major Projects—Two weeks prior to change date.
  2) Nonemergency—Five days prior to change date.
  3) Emergency Fix—Submitted within 24 hours after the fix has been implemented.

7.4.2 Change Control List

Table 7–2 is used to determine what procedures/tasks need to be reported through the change control process for approval. There are different requirements for production and development environments. For the production environments, all procedures/tasks must go through change control except where noted "NOT REQ'D." In the development environment, only those procedures/tasks noted as "REQ'D" need to go through change control. All other items in the development environment do not need to follow the formal change control process.

Table 7–2   The Change Control List

Procedure/Task	Production	Development
application account add/change/delete	NOT REQ'D	
application mail changes	NOT REQ'D	
application patches (vendor software)		
application software installation		
application upgrades		
backups unscheduled requests		
concurrent manager add/delete		
database account add/change/delete	NOT REQ'D	
database creation		
database expansion		
database exports (special)		
database exports (standard)	NOT REQ'D	
database gzip start/stop		
database gzips (not through cron — manual runs)		
database imports		
database indexes rebuild	NOT REQ'D	
database moves		
database ongoing purging	NOT REQ'D	
database purges special/initial		
database start/stop		
database table defrag	NOT REQ'D	
database tuning		
hardware repairs		REQ'D
hardware upgrades		REQ'D
links adds/drops		
modify /etc/system file		
modify alarms		REQ'D
modify automounts		
modify backup/gzip schedules		

Table 7–2   The Change Control List (Continued)

Procedure/Task	Production	Development
modify crontab – application		
modify crontab – dba	NOT REQ'D	
modify crontab – system		
modify init.ora		
modify log purges		
modify oracle listeners/tnsnames		
modify purge scripts		
modify UNIX scripts		
monitor tools add/change/delete		
network changes		REQ'D
new plants/factories		
OS tuning		REQ'D
OS upgrades		REQ'D
paging add/change/delete	NOT REQ'D	
PE installation		
PE patches		
printer add/change/delete		
printer jobs cancellation	NOT REQ'D	
printer start/stop	NOT REQ'D	
reboot servers		
refresh brando application software		REQ'D
system maintenance		
tape creation (special)		REQ'D
tape creation (standard)	NOT REQ'D	
UNIX account add/change/delete	NOT REQ'D	
UNIX mail changes	NOT REQ'D	

Structuring for Success

▶ 8.1 Introduction

In Chapter 6 we laid out the steps for development of the service model, the foundation of the Integrated Service Delivery (ISD). Chapter 8 builds on the service model, using it to determine the skill sets needed to support the customers. In developing the work packages for the service model, we grouped the services by a specific type of skill set. This now allows us to develop job descriptions that can be aligned with each work package.

▶ 8.2 Structuring the Organization

One of the goals in developing the ISD organization was to create opportunities for movement within the organization. We tried not to develop the traditional organizational structure, where division of labor is based on job function. Instead, our goal was to create an organization that had loose boundaries between job functions. We wanted to establish career paths that enabled our employees to grow into new job functions, if they wished, without having to leave the organization.

To aid in our goal of retaining employees, we developed a career path diagram to show people their paths for advancement. A career path diagram (Figure 8–1) shows how we created career advancement within a particular job such as systems administrator. The systems administrator can advance from entry-level to senior-level position. Our objective here was to enable our technical staff to stay within a particular job function and still be able to advance. The old school of thought for job advancement was to move into management positions in order to move up in pay scale. Instead, with technical resource in demand in the marketplace, we needed to create a career path within a job function that would allow us to retain employees that did not want a management career. Creating multiple levels allowed us to increase the pay scale without mandating a career movement into management.

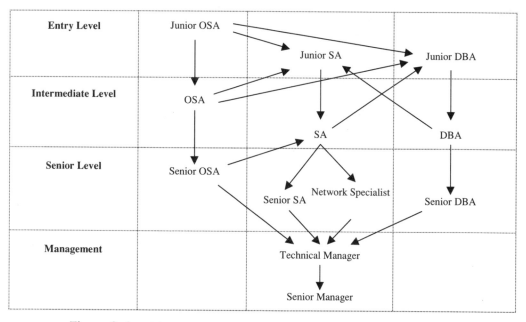

Figure 8–1 ISD career paths.

We also have career paths for individuals who are seeking a change in their responsibilities in the technical field. In the ISD organization, employees have the opportunity of switching job functions if they desire. For example, there is a career path from an Oracle database administrator (DBA) to a systems administrator (SA). The boundaries of each job have tasks assigned to them that cross into the traditional role that these jobs once had. For example, the systems administrators need experience on Oracle databases in order to carry out responsibilities such as monitoring, shutdowns, testing, and scripting. In the past, when database problems occurred, such as startup failures, the DBA would be called immediately. With the responsibilities for some database tasks now within the SA job function, the SA gains knowledge of Oracle database administration functions that could enable them to seek a position as a DBA if they wish. It also enables cross-training of the ISD teams.

8.2.1 Help Desk

The help desk was another area in which we took a nontraditional approach. Instead of creating a tier I type help desk job position with the main responsibility of call answering and forwarding, we added the help desk responsibility to that of the Oracle systems administrator job function. We envisioned that the Oracle systems administrators would rotate part-time duty on the help desk, four to eight hours a week. We did this for several reasons.

We viewed the help desk area as an area of high turnover. Most help desk candidates are recent college graduates looking for experience that allows them to advance into another position that better matches their career goals. Not too many college graduates want to become a help desk analyst. By adding the job responsibilities of a typical help desk role into the Oracle systems administrator (OSA) job responsibilities, we are attempting to reduce the turnover rate by providing a more challenging position with potential to advance into other technical areas. Our goal is to keep these people in the organization. Any time we have to retrain new employees is not only expensive, but, more importantly, it usually leads to reduced customer satisfaction during the initial months of training.

Customer satisfaction was an important reason for adding the help desk responsibilities to the OSAs. We wanted our help desk to be more than a call response center. Our goal is to answer as many customers' questions on the first call. This means the help desk needs to be experienced in tier I and tier II type questions. One way to get this experience is to perform the tasks and responsibilities that provide them with the necessary experience. Having help desk personnel (Oracle systems administrators) answer phones four to eight hours a week, gives them the majority of their work week to get hands-on experience. An associated goal was to get the help desk personnel out with the customer, to meet them face-to-face and see the real problems firsthand.

Finally, many of the tasks assigned to the Oracle systems administrator could be performed during slow periods while answering help desk phones. This is especially true during the second and third shift when the call volume is reduced. We wanted to try and keep the help desk personnel productive when call volumes were low.

8.2.2 Job Descriptions

As part of the ISD organization, we have a career document package for each employee. The package contains the career path diagram, discussed earlier in this section, and job descriptions for each position offered within the organization. This not only outlines the expectations of jobs held by employees, but also shows the options available to the employee.

Each job description lists the qualifications based on education, work experience, and necessary job skills. It outlines the detailed responsibilities for each job. The responsibilities can be mapped back to the work packages created in the service model. Finally, the job description sets in place the training and development goals of the position. Detailed job descriptions are developed for each level of a job function: junior, intermediate, and senior.

Job descriptions are based on the service work packages associated with the service model. Nine job functions (positions) were created at Xerox Corporation to support the service model in place. Listed below are the nine generic job positions. Many of the jobs have the junior, intermediate, and senior levels associated with them.

Here is a list of the positions available within the ISD organization:

Administrative Assistant (AA)

Operations Support Clerk (OSC)

Database Administrator (DBA)

Oracle System Administrator (OSA)

Manager (Mgr)

System Administrator (SA)

Network Specialist (NS)

Customer Support Manager (CS Mgr)

Operations Manager (Ops Mgr)

Detailed job descriptions for each of these positions can be found in Appendix A.

Resource and Cost Model

▶ 9.1 Introduction

▶ 9.1 Introduction

Chapter 6 showed us how to develop the service model based on the creation of work packages that support the services being requested from customers. In Chapter 8 we developed job descriptions, which were aligned to the work packages in the service model. Chapter 9 centers around the resource model, which combines the work packages and job descriptions to provide an approach to estimate the number of people needed to support customer requests. It also helps in determining the number and type of resources required; that is, one Jr. DBA, three intermediate DBAs, and two Sr. DBAs. The end result of the resource model is to estimate the number of hours needed to support work packages. The model helps justify the work effort needed to support the customers. From the resource model we feed the information into a cost model to estimate the labor cost associated with the service model.

9.2   Resource Model

The resource model combines the work packages and job descriptions to provide an approach to estimate the number of people needed to support customer requests. To develop the resource model we used a spreadsheet. The work packages from the service model make up the rows, and the job titles from the job description make up the columns. In addition to the job titles, there are several new columns added to aid in estimating the hours for each work package.

- Scheduled or On Demand
- Offered Time
- Skill Set
- Frequency
- Unit of Measure

9.2.1   Scheduled or On Demand

Scheduled or On Demand is a determination of when the service is performed. A scheduled service would be a work package that is performed on an ongoing basis. Server monitoring and database monitoring are examples of scheduled services because they must be performed periodically without being requested by the customer. Server installation and software installation are examples of on-demand services. The ISD organization would only perform these services when requested by the customer.

9.2.2   Offered Time

Offered Time is a determination of the time period the service is offered. Most ISD organizations are 24 hours by seven days (24 × 7) operations. But not all services are performed anytime, every day of the week. Many services are dependent on customers being available to assist in the request. There are two time periods used in the resource model: 24 × 7 and 8 × 5 (eight hours, Monday–Friday). An attempt is also made to determine if the 24 × 7 time offering can be supported via pager or does the resource needs to be on-site. For example, the help desk work package is usually offered as 24 × 7 and supported by on-site ISD employees. This is necessary to provide a timely response to customer calls. On the other hand, service performance tuning is a 24 × 7 service offering, but can be supported by an on-call person via pager. It is not necessary to have resources on-site 24 × 7 waiting for a server to be tuned. If a performance problem arises, there should be sufficient time for a person to be paged and adjust a tuning parameter. Determining the offering time will help to estimate the amount of hours required supporting the work package.

9.2.3 Skill Set

Skill Set is the job description code assigned to this work package. For example, "DBA" code is for database administrator and "Jr. SA" code is for junior system administrator. Even though the job titles are displayed as columns across the spreadsheet, this column assists in showing what work package is associated with the job title. Since the spreadsheet can get large, this column provides a quick reference.

9.2.4 Frequency

Frequency is how many times a work package will be performed. To determine frequency you need to examine the "Schedule or On Demand," "Offered Time," and "Unit of Measurement" columns. These columns will give you an indication of how to estimate the frequency. For example, the service installation work package has been determined to be "on demand," with an offered time of 8 × 5 and a unit of measure of one. Based on this information, frequency should be estimated on how many server installations will be requested by your customers. If the estimate is 15 server installs, 15 is the frequency number placed in this column.

Let's look at another example. The server backup work package is "scheduled" with an offering time of 24 × 7 on-site and a unit of measure of a "day." Server backups must occur every day, are scheduled to occur seven days a week, and could take place anytime during the day. Knowing this information, the frequency for server backups is 365 (days), because the ISD organization will need to ensure backups every day of the year.

9.2.5 Unit of Measure

Unit of Measure determines how the work package will be measured. There are several units of measure that can be used. A day, week, month, or year can be a measure of unit, or it could also be measured as a unit of one. For example, if you are estimating time for the installation of a server, the unit of measure should be one. It's best to use units of measure of one when the work package can be estimated by counting the number of activities. Work packages such as server installations, database creations, and number of help desk calls, are all services that can be measured in a unit of one. For example, 10 server installations a year, 20 database creations, and 10,000 help desk calls are estimates that can be given.

Work packages that are ongoing, scheduled type services should be measured by a time period such as a day, week, or month. Work packages such as cost management and server performance monitoring are an example of work packages that need to be measured in time periods. These are ongoing activities that need to be provided throughout the life of the support agreement.

Estimating the number of server units can be tricky because all servers are not equal. Servers can be either all from one vendor or a combination of several different vendors. Each of these servers has different complexities. The goal is to develop a unit of measure that is consistent between all servers. The section below shows us how to develop a rating system to determine the number of units.

▶ 9.3 Estimating Server Units

ISD organizations support many physical servers. As mentioned, the servers can be all from one vendor or a combination of several different vendors. They are not all equal. For example, a SUN E10K server requires a great deal more time to set up as compared to a SUN Ultra 1 server. A Compaq file server will probably be installed with a different operating system than a Sequent server. The time allocation for setup and installation of the servers will be different. It would not be correct to allocate the same amount of time for each physical server. The goal is to determine a base unit of one that can be used in the resource model to estimate total time allocated to a work package. In the end, there might be 70 physical servers being supported, but only 53 units used in the calculation of time resource.

Units of one can be accomplished by a rating system. All servers independent of the vendor can be rated together. The rating system for servers is a judgmental decision based on experience, vendor estimates, and benchmarking data. Start by determining a server type/size that will be the foundation server that is equal to a unit of one. Then, judge each other's different type server against this foundation server.

For example, if we determine a SUN E5000/E6000 server is equal to one unit, each other SUN server type is compared to the SUN E5000/E6000. What is being compared is the amount of time that it takes to complete tasks such as server setup/installation, software loading, system monitoring, and problem resolution. A SUN Ultra 1, Ultra 5, and Ultra 10, is judged to be ¼ of a unit, a SUN SPARC 1000/2000 is ¾ of a unit, and an E10K is 4 units of the E5000/E6000. A chart of the SUN server types would be as follows:

Sun Server type/size	Units Compared to Foundation server
E10K	4 units
E5000/E6000	1 unit
Sparc 1000/2000	¾ unit
E250/E450	½ unit
Ultra series	¼ unit
Sparc 5 and 10	¼ unit

To determine the number of units of one to be used in the resource model, just multiply the number of servers in each type/size to the unit rating. In the example below there are 34 physical servers, but only 24 units.

Sun Server type/size	Units Compared to Foundation server	Number of Servers	Total Units
E10K	4 units	2	8
E5000/E6000	1 unit	7	7
Sparc 1000/2000	¾ unit	9	7 rounded
E250/E450	½ unit	0	0
Ultra series	¼ unit	14	4 rounded
Sparc 5 and 10	¼ unit	12	3

		Total Units	29

▶ 9.4 Resource Spreadsheet

Figures 9–1, 9–2, and 9–3 are examples of three work packages shown in the spreadsheet model. The rows of the spreadsheet are the individual work packages from the service model. In Figure 9–1, we have chosen to display each task underneath the work package title. This helps determine the estimate of hours for each work package by giving a reminder of what the total work package consists of. You can choose to display only the work package title.

In addition to the five columns described previously, you can see there are two additional columns for each job position within the ISD organization. One column is used to estimate the hour (sometimes minutes) needed to complete the work package based on the unit of measure. The second column, "Total xx," calculates the hour's estimate times for the unit of measure for that job position. You will also notice instead of listing each junior, intermediate, and senior level of a job position in the columns, we listed only the generic job title. For example, we have only a column for "SA Effort Hrs," and not additional columns for Jr. SA, Intermediate SA, and Sr. SA. Instead, we use the "Skill Set" column to distinguish the different levels within a job position. Let's now examine each of the decisions made for these three work packages.

9.5 Cost Management

Service	Sched or On Dmnd	Offered	Skill Set	Freq	UOM	......	Clerk Effort Hrs / UOM	Total Clerk	.....
	S	5x8	Sr. Clerk	260	Days		2	520	
Maintain chargeback model									
Ensure new transfer agreements in place									
Renew yearly transfer agreements									
Ensure revenue received from customers									
Cost reporting to customer and management									

Figure 9–1   Cost management.

Sched or On Dmnd   The "S" indicator states that this work package is slated to be performed on a routine (scheduled) basis. The determination was made because cost tracking needs to be performed on a regular basis to maintain books. There are cost reports that need to be prepared and distributed to the customers monthly. Even though there is a task, "Renew yearly transfer agreements," these agreements must be worked throughout the year in order to ensure the correct amount of money is being allocated and agreed upon.

Offered   This work package is performed (offered) five days a week, Monday–Friday, eight hours a day. This is not to say the work package will be worked 40 hours a week (8 × 5 = 40), but only that it should be performed sometime during this period. Cost management is a task that does not require off-hour support, therefore the determination of 8 × 5.

Skill Set   Since this work package is centered around maintaining costs, tracking agreements, and preparing reports, we determine that a Sr. Clerk position would be appropriate. Our assumption here was that one of the management positions would be responsible for setting up the initial cost schedule and that the transfer agreements would be in place. This position would only be responsible for maintaining these items.

Freq Since this work package is offered 8 × 5, the frequency was determined to be 260 days. That is the average number of workdays in a year.

UOM This work package will be estimated based on the number of hours in a day that is needed to support cost management. The "day" unit was chosen because this is an ongoing type of support function that, on average, has time spent on its activity each day.

Clerk Effort Hrs/UOM For the Cost Management work packages we estimate two hours a day would be spent on these tasks, based on the number of customers we support and the associated number of transfer agreements we have to maintain.

Total Clerk This is a calculation of the frequency column (260) times the Clerk Effort Hrs column (2) which equals 560 hours. This is the estimate of the total hours per year that we projected would be spent on this work package.

▶ ## 9.6 Ongoing DB Monitoring and Maintenance

Service	Sched or On Dmnd	Offered	Skill Set	Freq	UOM	......	DBA Effort Hrs / UOM	Total DBA	.....
	S	24x7 Pager	Junior DBA	60	DBs		40	2400	
Database activity									
Concurrent manager activity									
ORASRV process alive and well									
Listener server alive and well									
Monitor for down databases									
Monitor for down concurrent managers									

Figure 9–2 Ongoing DB monitoring and maintenance.

Sched or On Dmnd The "S" indicator states that this work package is slated to be performed on a routine (scheduled) basis. This work package does have "on demand" type of activities in that it supports databases seven days, 24 hours a day, by pager. In this case a determi-

Chapter **9** I Resource and Cost Model

nation was made that the off-hour pager support would not be the norm. If we were successful in performing database monitoring on a regular basis, then off-hours support calls should be low. Therefore, we deem this to be a scheduled work package.

Offered Because ISD maintains production databases that are operational 7 days a a week, 24 hours a day, this work package needs to be offered during that time range.

Skill Set A Jr. DBA has been slotted to be responsible for this work package. This determination was made because the monitoring is well documented. There are procedures in place for each individual event monitoring routine that is executed against a database. There are also suggested corrective actions documented to help fix problems. An Intermediate or Senior DBA is not needed (but may help out when needed) to perform this scheduled work package. This work package is also a good learning vehicle to help train a junior person.

Freq In this example, UOM is a database. Frequency is the estimated number of databases that would be supported. In this example, 60 databases were estimated to be supported by the ISD organization.

UOM Database monitoring and maintenance is proportional to the number of databases being supported. For each database, we need to spend "x" amount of hours on this work package. Because of this, we determined that the unit of measure is a database.

Jr. DBA Effort Hrs/UOM An estimate of 40 hours a year would be required on each database to monitor and maintain it. This might seem low, but in this estimate many of the 60 databases (frequency) are identical. They are copies of the same database, used for different purposes. Copies of databases are made to support development, testing, training, software patching, and sandbox use. Having the database identical in structure cuts down the number of hours needed to monitor and maintain each database. In theory, if we see problems in one database, identical copies of that database should be having the same problems. This cuts down the need to analyze and resolve problems. Do it once, apply it multiple times.

Total Jr. DBA This is a calculation of the frequency column (60) times the Jr. DBA Effort Hrs column (40) that equals 2400 hours. This is the estimate of the total hours per year that we projected would be spent on this work package.

▶ 9.7 Application Server Support

Service	Sched or On Dmnd	Offered	Skill Set	Freq	UOM	......	SA Effort Hrs / UOM	Total SA	.....
	O/D	8x5	SA	260	Days		9	2340	
Assist in software installs / upgrade									
Assist in creation of scheduling jobs									
Directory setup									
Application tuning									
Job monitoring									
Mount tapes on servers as required									

Figure 9–3 Application server support.

Sched or On Dmnd The "O/D" indicator states that this work package is slated to be performed on demand. Tasks in this work package are usually requested by the developers, DBAs, and customers to be performed at a certain time. The requests are based on their project schedule.

Offered These tasks can be performed during normal working hours and need the assistance of the requester to be completed, which is usually between the hours of 8 A.M. and 5 P.M. when the customers are at work. Although some requests may be performed during off-hours, a determination was made to offer this work package 8 × 5, since the majority of it can be completed M–F, 8–5.

Skill Set The tasks represented in this work package vary in responsibility skill level. At times you may want a Sr. SA to perform an upgrade of software that is mission critical, but you may allow a Jr. SA to perform a software upgrade on a test server for the experience. A Jr. SA should easily accomplish tasks such as job monitoring and tape mounts. Because of the wide range of skill sets, we slotted this skill set for an Intermediate SA, shown as SA.

Freq We set the frequency at 260 days. Because of the large number of servers being supported (greater than 50), we determined that requests for support on these tasks would happen on a daily basis. If we had the same number of servers (less than 25), we might have determined the frequency and UOM based on the number of servers.

UOM Because of the large number of servers and the random on-demand type of requests for support of these tasks, we determined that days would best fit as a unit of measure. It would be much easier to estimate how many hours a day might be required to complete this work package, then estimate by the number of servers.

SA Effort Hrs/UOM An estimate of nine hours a day would be required to support this work package. This was based on the large amount of servers and customers (developers, DBAs, and end customers) being supported.

Total SA This is a calculation of the frequency column (260) times the SA Effort Hrs column (9) that equals 2340 hours. This is the estimate of the total hours per year that we projected would be spent on this work package.

In summary, the end result of the resource model is to estimate the number of hours needed to support work packages. The columns—Schedule or On Demand, Offered, Skill Set, Frequency, and Unit of Measure—are there to help you derive an estimate. After using this tool and arriving at an estimate, you need to "stand back" and place a mental check on the results as a sanity check. If the estimate seems low or high based on your knowledge of the environment being supported, it probably is. Go back into the resource model and make adjustments until it feels right. The resource model is a tool to help justify the work effort needed to support the customers. It also helps in determining the number and type of resources required, that is, one Jr. DBA, three intermediate DBAs, and two Sr. DBAs. You should review the resource model on a periodic basis and make changes based on new information.

▶ 9.8   Cost Model

The cost model takes the total hours from the resource model and determines the resource head count for each position in the ISD organization. Then it applies the estimated cost for each resource to calculate the labor cost of the organization. Table 9–1 shows an example of a cost model.

Table 9–1   Cost Model

	SA	OSA	DBA	Clerical	Network	Manager
Staff Year Hrs	2,080	2,080	2,080	2,080	2,080	2,080
Productivity Rate	0.80	0.80	0.80	0.80	0.80	0.80
Vacation Hrs	40	40	40	40	40	40
Training Hrs	40	40	40	40	40	40
Sick Hrs	16	16	16	16	16	16
Workable Hrs	1,568	1,568	1,568	1,568	1,568	1,568
Cost per FTE	$100,000	$50,000	$110,000	$30,000	$130,000	$140,000
Total Effort Hrs	12,450	8,450	15,235	1,825	1,100	1,950
Raw Resources Needed	7.940	5.389	9.716	1.164	0.702	1.244
Rounded	8	6	10	1	1	2
Avg. Cost	$800,000	$300,000	$1,100,000	$30,000	$130,000	$280,000

Totals

Raw Resources	= 26.15433673
Rounded Resources	= 27
Estimated Costs	= $2,640,000

At the top of the cost model is the job position from the resource model. Notice: Even though in the resource model we tried to determine the level (senior, intermediate, or junior) of the resource, in this example of the cost model we use the generic resource title. We chose to calculate cost on an average of a resource, instead of estimating the cost of a senior, intermediate, and junior position of the job. You can take the model to another level of detail by adding columns for each level of resource and determining the head count and costs of each. But, since the cost model is an estimate, going to this level of detail might not be worth the effort. In the end, the cost of hiring each resource will vary.

Staff Year Hours   The staffed year hour's row is the total number of workable hours in a year. This was determined by multiplying 52 work weeks times five days a week, times eight hours a day to get 2080 hours per year.

Productivity Rate   This is a determination for the amount of time a resource can be productive in an eight-hour day. For this example we are using a 80 percent productivity rate.

Vacation Hours This is the average number of hours being allotted to each resource per year for vacation time.

Training Hours This is the average number of hours being allotted to each resource per year for training.

Sick Hours This is the estimate of the average number of hours allotted to each resource per year for sick time.

Workable Hours This is a calculation of the total hours a year a resource will be available to work on tasks in the service model. This is determined by taking the staff years times the productivity rate, minus vacation, training, and sick hours. Example:

$$2,080 \times .80 = 1,664 - 40 = 1,624 - 40 = 1,584 - 16 = 1,568$$

Cost per FTE Cost per full-time equivalent is the estimated average cost for each resource.

Total Effort Hours This is the number of hours calculated from the resource model.

Raw Resources This is a calculation for the number of resources needed to support a job title. This is determined by dividing the workable hours by the total effort hours from the resource model.

Rounded This is the whole number of resources needed to support a job title.

Average Cost This is a calculation for the number of rounded resources times the cost of FTE.

Benchmarking

Modern benchmarking evolved from the work done by R.C. Camp at Xerox, which is well documented in his 1989 book, *Benchmarking*. Benchmarking is generally defined as measuring your own products, services, and practices against the best in the field. It is often used as a precursor to reengineering efforts. Identifying best-of-breed processes and metrics to measure those processes is the typical goal of benchmarking efforts.

Classic benchmarking efforts oriented to manufacturing type environments can often be quite extensive, exhaustive, and expensive. In the rapidly changing and evolving IT environment, time is of the essence and return on investment is often challenging to calculate. Applying a focused approach while retaining primary process steps is the key to successfully implementing benchmarking in an ISD environment. The primary process steps are:

- Establish the reason to benchmark
- Develop an understanding of the current environment's needs
- Identify appropriate target companies
- Develop a methodology of collecting information
- Commit to a plan of utilizing the information collected

Benchmarking is a viable tool to use in the development of an ISD environment.

10.1 Why Benchmark?

Establishing a reason to go through the time and expense of benchmarking is essential. If operations management, IT management, and the team performing the benchmarking are not convinced that the results will be utilized, the efforts will be in vain.

10.1.1 Understanding the Current Environment

While much of benchmarking is focused externally, the initial steps should be internally oriented. The old planning adage of, "if you don't know where you are going, any road will take you there," is essential in setting direction and establishing plans; but equally important is the adage, "if you don't know where you are, a map won't help you."

Benchmarking should begin with a comprehensive review or assessment of the current environment. This should not be confused with defining the service requirements that the organization may have. Nor should the focus of this effort be oriented toward operations improvement. The focus should be developing a base of knowledge of the current environment that will serve as a navigation guide going forward in creating the infrastructure necessary to deliver the services required.

10.1.2 Get New Ideas

A criticism of benchmarking in the past is that it is more imitative in nature than innovative. By mimicking each other, the argument goes that there will be an averaging down of corporate capabilities driven by the law of diminishing marginal returns.

There is no evidence that leveraging off of an existing level of knowledge and expertise produces fewer "breakthrough concepts" than independent, isolated, and insulated think tank environments. An argument can be made that all innovation is triggered or stimulated by some bit of information that currently exists in some form.

The act of reviewing or assessing the current environment addressed above will most likely stimulate many new ideas. Adding the stimulus of external sources of information, knowledge, and expertise should definitely produce at least a rainstorm, if not a monsoon, of fresh ideas.

10.1.3 Ratify Old Ideas

New ideas are not always the best ideas in a given situation, organization, or time frame. Finding that services, processes, and technologies utilized in other firms are comparable to either the existing environment or the target environment give management comfort and confidence that they are not too far off the mark and may move forward at an accelerated pace.

▶ 10.2 Establishing a Company Profile

Benchmarking is frequently described as being tactically oriented or focused. To derive the maximum benefit from any benchmarking effort, a strategic, cultural, and organizational profile should be developed. This more strategic-oriented profile, the tactically oriented assessment (addressed above), and the service requirements will form the framework to insure the most effective capture of the right data from the right firm.

The analysis of the benchmark data will be totally ineffective without the delineating information contained in a company profile. Much of the information to be incorporated into a company profile may already exist in some form or context within the organization and need only be pulled into a model that can be used as a tool.

This profile can exist in the form of a checklist, a summary of statements, or an annotated graphic that describes how the company views itself.

10.2.1 Understand Business Context

An earlier section described the need to create a linkage between the business mission and IT services being provided to support and enable business activities. Integrating this information into the framework that will be used to guide the collection, analysis, and implementation of benchmark data is a key to success in this phase of creating a comprehensive integrated service delivery capability.

Maintaining an ongoing business focus during all phases will ensure that the services measured against and ultimately delivered will support management's objectives and therefore be much easier to market and communicate.

A review of business objectives and the services that are currently supporting these objectives will be a worthwhile exercise in conjunction with profiling the company with the benchmarking effort.

10.2.2 Key on Primary Areas of Concern, Vulnerability, or Exposure

Identify corporate hot buttons or vulnerabilities that need to be addressed or quarantined. In addition to understanding and integrating strategies and objectives into the benchmarking process, reviewing current operating measures and performance metrics should be an integral part of building the company profile.

Being aware of current and potential problem areas will ensure that a concentrated effort will be made to collect data that will assist in creating services that will combat the noted vulnerabilities or problems.

10.2.3 Understand Yourself

Understand the cultural resistance to change, tolerance for risk, and other nonlinear measures. Benchmarking often focuses narrowly on metrics and specific processes. Be aware and sensitive to soft issues. Internally, such areas as satisfaction with existing IT services, the tendency to contract out services, and the frequency of change are indicators that should be referenced during the benchmarking effort. Inspecting the change management process and records can provide invaluable clues as to who is sensitive to what issues at certain times.

Looking at what others perceive to be sensitive and vulnerable in the organization can also be a worthwhile exercise.

In addition to answering the questionnaire developed to aid in data collection at target sites, a general assessment that broadly views all the data center functions will be very helpful.

The following is an outline of a basic assessment tool:

Data Center Assessment

- Data Center Management
  - How are service levels agreed to and monitored?
  - How is the data center organized to produce optimum service?
  - What is the skill level of the staff?
  - How do the physical facilities support service delivery?
  - What type of documentation facilitates ongoing operations?

- Change Management
  - How are changes to systems effected and communicated?
  - How are emergency changes handled?
  - What processes are in effect to certify or validate changes prior to being put into production?

- Problem Management
  - How are problems identified, documented, tracked, and resolved?
  - What are the functions of the help desk?
  - What types of quality incentives are in place?

- Data Management
  - What type of backup and restore policies and procedures are in place?
  - What are the standard storage configurations?
  - How is data media storage handled?

- Software Management
  - How is software version control maintained?
  - What criteria are utilized to measure the acceptability of software for production?

— What support is required for application development environments?

- Network Management
  — How is the network monitored?
  — What are the network availability requirements?
  — How is network expansion managed?

- Capacity and Performance
  — How is resource utilization measured?
  — What performance metrics are in place?
  — How are capacity requirements forecasted?

- Security
  — What security policies are in place and how are they enforced?
  — How is external access to systems controlled?
  — How are intrusions detected and investigated?

- Disaster Recovery
  — How does the disaster recovery plan work?
  — How does the IT architecture facilitate disaster prevention and facilitate recovery?
  — How is the testing of disaster recovery plans handled?

- Asset Management
  — How are asset inventories maintained?
  — What are the procurement policies and procedures?
  — How are charges for service accounted for?

10.3 Identifying Target Companies

Benchmarking against one or two conveniently or attractively located peers may be the easiest path to secure volunteer assistance and the quickest way to obtain data. However, easy and quick don't often lead to quality. Objectively and deliberately analyzing the potential targets for benchmarking will produce results that will generate the best ROI or most gain for the pain.

10.3.1 Identify Peers

In most instances companies are aware of who their peers are, often painfully so in the case of competitors. The key is to identify those peers that most closely reflect the same image the company profile projects in terms of vulnerabilities, concerns, and cultural issues. Of course, the company must offer the majority of the services that have been identified as being required to support the company's business activities and enable the accomplishment of the enterprise's mission.

IT operations and senior management, as well as the marketing/sales staff, are great sources for lists of potential benchmarking candidates.

There will be a natural tendency to gravitate toward peers in the same industry. Firms outside your industry that offer the same or similar IT services and generally fit your company profile may be an excellent source of innovative ideas that have been born in a totally different environment.

10.3.2 Utilize Vendor's Resources

Vendors often have a vast amount of data and market intelligence that can be leveraged in the benchmarking process. In addition to assisting, discretely, in identifying firms to benchmark against, some vendors such as Sun Microsystems can serve as a benchmark since they operate a multifaceted, multinational, multibillion dollar corporation that is supported by an excellent internal IT organization.

If your vendor of choice also runs their enterprise on their equipment, generally fits the company profile, and offers similar services, a wealth of information can be available on an as-needed basis or provided via their professional services organization.

10.3.3 Coordinate Data Collection/Visits

Showing up unannounced at a firm you wish to benchmark against will probably not generate much in the way of results, but will likely generate embarrassment and ill will. As in most endeavors, whether house painting or benchmarking, preparation and planning is the key to success.

Once the target firms have been identified as described above, coordinating and often negotiating data collection is next. The following steps can increase the probability of obtaining the necessary data relatively painlessly:

- Initial contact should be at the highest level within IT as possible—ideally, the CIO.

- Contact should be made by a peer or at least a representative of a peer; "Mr. CIO of our firm asked me to contact you."

- Once a contact has been made and an agreement to serve as a benchmark is reached, appropriate management/staff—data center manager, IT controller, etc.—should be identified and available to participate.

- A questionnaire that covers all the services to be covered in the benchmarking effort should be developed and forwarded to the target company in advance.

- When travel restrictions, scheduling conflicts, or other impediments stand in the way of a physical visit, a structured and facilitated teleconference can produce satisfactory, if not optimum, results.

Learn about the firm prior to the site visit. By doing so, the individuals that will participate in the meeting can use relevant industry data to increase their probability of securing the optimum amount of information.

10.3.4   Sensitivity to Peer Sites

When invited into the inner sanctum of an IT organization, you must always be sensitive to how you react if you are in a less than optimum environment. Regardless of how carefully and diligently target sites are selected, some may not be good fits in some or all areas. Remember that every experience serves a useful purpose, even if it is only to be an example of what not to do.

The most likely outcome of the site visits will be that the sum total of all the visits, not one or two sites alone, will provide the data and value desired.

10.3.5 Confidentiality

In the case of vendors, a non-disclosure agreement may be the order of the day to mutually protect valuable information and intellectual properties. Such agreements probably are not appropriate or required if a good measure of common sense and corporate integrity are exercised.

A variation of the golden rule may be a good guide: Don't ask for or take any information from a benchmark site that you would not be willing to give out.

10.4 Developing Your Questionnaire

A key element of the benchmarking process is the questionnaire. Properly constructed, it will provide a guide to efficiently capturing the data necessary to validate the service delivery direction and leverage off of existing knowledge and expertise.

10.4.1 Structure Queries Appropriately

Asking questions about services that you are not permitted to offer or that can be answered with a yes or no response will yield very marginal results. In addition to specific service-focused questions, open-ended questions such as, "If you could change any part of your service delivery arena, what would it be and why?" should be sprinkled throughout the site visit.

A team approach to site visits is an excellent method to reduce the strain on one person having to ask questions, document, and observe simultaneously. Ideally, team members with complementary knowledge and expertise is useful.

10.4.2 Site Visit Questionnaire

The following is a preamble to a questionnaire used in a benchmarking effort focused on creating an ISD environment. The actual questionnaire is included below the preamble.

A customer is in the process of developing and evaluating alternative approaches to providing an efficiently run infrastructure to support new client server applications being developed within the enterprise. The target environment will consist of UNIX database servers, NT Citrix servers, Oracle manufacturing and financial applications, and PC desktops.

In order to ensure that comparable data is captured and everyone's time is efficiently utilized, we would appreciate your reviewing the following questions prior to our visit.

GENERAL

What are the major or key applications running in your data center?

How many data centers are there?

What is the total number of users supported by the data center(s)?

Are service level agreements in place?

What type of service level metrics are utilized?

What is the level of process documentation?

What is the level of TQM/Process Improvement programs operating?

What is the level of outsourcing/insourcing?

How are the production, development, and testing environments different?

Is the data center a 7 × 24 × 365 operation?

FINANCIAL

What is the total IT budget?

What is the data center budget?

Is there a chargeback system?

What is the basis of the cost chargeback distribution?

What is the average cost per user, IT seat?

How are technology assets accounted for?

What tools are used to account for assets?

What cost reduction efforts or consolidations have taken place or been planned?

How are major infrastructure projects funded?

ORGANIZATION/STAFFING

What are the functional units that comprise IT?

What are the functional unit's basic responsibilities?

What is the number of IT staffing per functional unit?

How many levels of organizations from CIO to lowest level IT staff?

What is the cost of developing/maintaining staff skills?

How are skill sets and tasks balanced in small sites or in off shifts?

What does the organization chart look like? Copy?

What is the level of turnover?

What is the primary cause of turnover?

How is training administered?

What is the cost of training per employee?

HELP DESK

Where is it organizationally?

What are its functions?

What is its scope of responsibilities—desktop, applications, network?

Is it 7 × 24?

How is it staffed—allocation of resources over shifts, etc.?

What is the ratio of help desk to users supported?

What is the volume of help desk calls?

What percentage of calls are successfully closed by the help desk?

Where are the remainders of calls passed?

Who performs second- and third-level support?

Who tracks calls to closure?

What is the ratio of SAs to users supported?

How is call escalation handled?

What tools are used in the call center?

DATA CENTER

What is the size (sq ft) of the data center(s)?

What network management tools are being used?

What system management tools are being used?

How much processing power (MIPS), is in the data center?

How many GB of storage are in the data center?

How many printers are driven by the data center?

How many network connections are supported?

What is the level of power consumed by the data center?

How is capacity planned/managed?

What kinds of system management tools are used?

What kinds of network management tools are used?

CONTINGENCY/SECURITY

What types of contingency plans are in place?

How are disaster recovery plans tested?

What is the frequency of the tests?

How are environmental resources monitored?

What environmental monitoring tools are used?

How is physical, network, and software security administered?

What kinds of security monitoring tools are used?

SOFTWARE

How are new software releases moved into production?

How is version control managed?

How is data managed?

▶ 10.5 Analyzing the Benchmark Data

Expending the energy and expense of collecting information can all be for naught or generate only mediocre return on investment if the data is not converted into useful information that can be integrated into the overall service delivery creation process.

10.5.1 Document, Document, Document

Constructing great questionnaires, recruiting excellent team members, and conducting mind-expanding site visits will produce very little if there is no effective documentation created.

Assigning responsibility for documentation prior to the site visits is essential. That responsibility can be shared but, much like a successful marriage, each participant must contribute 100 percent, not a proportional percentage.

There may be an opportunity to do an audio or video recording of the site visit, but in many instances the presence of recording devices may dampen the spontaneity desired in the meeting.

Facility tours are especially useful to observe services actually being delivered, but are challenging from a documentation standpoint. A small notepad is very useful for this.

In addition to documenting the answers to the questionnaire, any documentation of processes, methods, agreements, or metrics are valuable artifacts to be collected.

10.5.2 Analyze Efficiently

Again, planning pays a premium in this aspect of benchmarking. In addition to using profiles, frameworks, and guidelines to keep the process focused, you must begin with the end in mind. Work backward and envision what it is you wish to prove or disprove about the service delivery environment and construct a process or methodology to accomplish that specifically. Create spreadsheets or shell databases in advance to aid in the analysis of the data captured.

Utilize research data from sources such as Gartner, Forrester, or Giga to supplement, enhance, and validate the data collected.

10.5.3 Be Quick or Be Dead

Getting caught up in analysis for the sake of analysis, or analysis paralysis, can produce a slow death to the benchmarking effort, as the value of the information has a very short half-life. Benchmarking information must be current, especially with the exponentially increasing rate of evolution or revolution that is taking place in the IT industry.

▶ 10.6 Implementation

Accepting the fact that benchmarking is useful, understanding the reasons to benchmark, identifying target benchmarking sites, and collecting and analyzing data will not generate one measure of value if information created out of the benchmarking effort is not integrated into the implementation of a world-class ISD infrastructure.

The benchmarking effort should not be an afterthought used to support decisions that already have been made; it should be an integral element in the overall service delivery creation process and follow right behind the service requirements definition in the sequence of steps.

Measuring Success

There is a small plaque that is on the wall in our kitchen. It reads, "When Mom ain't Happy, ain't Nobody Happy." Perhaps the plaque exhibits poor grammar, but it very succinctly communicates a message. The IT version of that plaque would read, "If the User isn't Happy, then Nobody is Happy." Going beyond this superficial cliché, understanding who "Mom" is in an IT context and that "happiness" is dynamic and can change at the click of a mouse is essential to being completely successful in constructing and implementing an enterprise ISD capability.

There are a myriad of techniques used to measure success: the balanced score approach described in an earlier chapter, the critical success factor approach, TQM, capability maturity model levels, and many others. The question to be asked is not what tool to use to measure success, but rather, how do you define success and who is the final arbiter of when success has been achieved?

▶ 11.1 Defining Success

The functional responsibility to understand who the consumer of IT services is and how they define success falls to the account management role in most IT organizations.

The charter of account management is to ensure that positive, constructive relationships are maintained between IT and its customers, develop service solutions, and manage the movement of service requests from initiation to implementation in support of business needs.

The general responsibilities of the account management function are:

- Ensure that a proactive, positive relationship is maintained between IT and users
- Provide a formalized planning process to ensure that current and future needs of business units are satisfied
- Ensure that all changes to the technology environment are authorized, analyzed, approved, implemented, and tracked in a timely, controlled manner
- Improve processes on an ongoing basis

11.1.1   Define Success Before You Start

In the IT service delivery arena "beginning with the end in mind" translates to understanding what the business needs are and how their satisfaction can be supported or enabled. Chapter 4, "Business Linkage," describes the path of linking the enterprise mission, strategies, and objectives to the IT services, and the people, processes, and technology that support/enable the satisfaction of those needs. Once the business needs are identified, a plan should be constructed to meet them.

Account planning should include the following steps or processes:

- Determine Business Needs
  The purpose of this procedure is to gain input into the account planning process with respect to changes that need to be factored into the business unit account plan and ultimately into the overall IT plan.

- Review Previous Experience
  The purpose of this procedure is to gain an understanding of the service history of a specific business unit user and provide a foundation to begin an account plan for them.

- Review Existing Service Level Agreements
  The purpose of this procedure is to review existing SLAs to determine where IT has performed admirably and poorly. The results of this review or audit will provide input into an account profile and evaluation of processes. The following is an outline of what should be included in an account profile. This profile should be maintained on an ongoing basis.
  — Business unit or subunit profiled
  — Applications supported and associated SLA
  — Other services provided
  — Composite or summary service satisfaction query responses
  — Service satisfaction survey responses
  — Service level agreement audit results
  — Gaps in service expectations and actual service provided
  — Future service needs

- Determine Satisfaction Level
  The purpose of this procedure is to develop a broad view of the overall satisfaction the user is experiencing from IT.

- Determine Expectations Gap
  The purpose of this procedure is to complete the account profile by analyzing the information contained in an account profile and highlight the gaps uncovered between the user's expectations and the service provided by IT.

- Develop Account Plan
  The purpose of this procedure is to create a document for each business unit that will serve as a focal point for planning how to provide service to that unit in the future. The following is an outline of an account plan:
  — Applications Supported
  — Services Provided
  — Service Improvements Required
    - Process Improvements Planned
    - Staffing/Training Plans
    - Technology Changes Planned
      — Hardware

- — Software
- — Network
- — Expansion/Contraction Predictions
  - Process Changes Planned
  - Staffing/Training Changes Planned
  - Technology Changes Planned
    - — Hardware
    - — Software
    - — Network
- — New Business Needs
  - New Process Requirements
  - Staffing/Training Requirements
  - Technology Requirements
    - — Hardware
    - — Software
    - — Network
- — Resource Changes Required for Business Unit for FY
  - Staffing/Training Requirements
  - Technology Requirements
    - — Hardware
    - — Software
    - — Network
- — Changes in Service Level Agreements Required

11.1.2 Service Level Agreements

The attributes of a service level agreement (SLA) was described in Chapter 5. The importance of an initial mutual agreement on what services are required to support applications cannot be underestimated.

Harris Kern, in his book *Rightsizing the New Enterprise*, provides an excellent description of the objectives of the SLA. The objective of the Service Level Agreement (SLA) is to define a framework for managing the quality and quantity of delivered services, in the face of changing business needs and user requirements, at a price the business is able to afford. Specifically, this document intends to:

- Synchronize IT services with the business needs of the customers
- Set the correct level of service expectations and responsibilities for both IT and the customer
- Enable IT to be an effective and flexible partner to the business unit, aiding rapid response to the changing business environment
- Enable IT to plan for the delivery of required services at the lowest cost to the customer
- Enable IT to maintain quality and visibility of the services that they can provide, and thus demonstrate value for money.[1]

You can find an example of SLA in Appendix B.

▶ 11.2 Ensuring Success

Devising an account management plan, defining success, and mutually agreeing to the definition via a service level agreement does not in and of itself guarantee success. The services identified in earlier chapters must be executed in an appropriate sequence and level of intensity. Much like the need for the account plan and service level agreement from a general standpoint, there is a need to "get in front of the curve" from a micro or individual application standpoint.

Sun Microsystems has created a process that ensures that operational services required to support and enable new applications during development, testing, and production are identified. This process is called the Client Server Production Acceptance (CSPA) process. A more detailed explanation of the CSPA process can be found in two books, *Managing the New Enterprise* and *Building the New Enterprise*. The process parallels and supports the application systems development methodology.

---

1. Harris Kern and Randy Johnson, *Rightsizing the New Enterprise*, SunSoft Press, 1994.

The CSPA consists of four phases:

Phase 1   Notification/Information Gathering

This phase provides a "heads up" to all parties that are impacted by the application and utilizes a comprehensive questionnaire to gather all the data necessary to define the skills, processes, and technology services required to support the development and operation of the new application.

A checklist is derived from this questionnaire that will be used to allocate tasks to the various roles that will be assigned responsibility for completion.

Examples of information to be gathered are:

- Server Strategy (Hardware)
  Server strategy—Where will the servers be located? Who will manage them?
- Server Strategy (Database)
  Database server strategy—How will the database, its backups, and its administration be accomplished?
- Client Strategy
  Client strategy—Where will the clients be located? Is there local support for these clients?
- Backup and Recovery
  What are the backup and recovery requirements? How will they be handled? Who will provide the service?
- Disaster Recovery Considerations
  How will recovery of the software application and its data be accomplished? Refer to a Disaster Recovery Architecture for guidelines.
- Uptime Requirements
  How many hours a day must the system be operational?
- International Considerations
  In what countries and during what time periods must the system operate?
- Licensing Mechanisms
  Define the licensing mechanisms(s) to be used (for licensed software).

Phase 2   Resource Planning /Communication

During this phase the necessary hardware, software, and other resources that will be required to generate the services are secured. Support of the application development and preparation for the production environment is the focus.

Phase 3   Implementation

During this phase all services that will be required to support the application are tested with the new application. The CSPA checklist is utilized as a tool to determine if the application and services supporting warrant a move to a production decision.

Phase 4   Maintenance and Support

The maintenance and support phase is an ongoing phase and is geared to insuring that the CSPA is kept current. Each time a change is required, the appropriate elements of the CSPA should be completed.

11.3   Metrics

In constructing the service model, an understanding of what the customer expects to be delivered will be negotiated, agreed to, and ultimately documented in a service level agreement. A key element of the SLA is defining the measures that will determine satisfaction of the agreement's terms. In fact, there may be layers of metrics that are not visible to the user, but support an overall measure of success. The metrics must not only be constructed to measure the success relative to a specific service and system's SLA, it must also be supportive of the overall business need that the IT service is supporting/enabling.

11.3.1   Service Level Definition

An initial step in establishing a set of metrics to measure and actually ensure success is to determine the level of service that must be provided by the functional service offering. Table 11–1 shows an example of a service level framework to use in determining the level of service that must be provided based on the system that is being supported.

Table 11–1   Service Level Framework

Service Level	Level 1	Level 2	Level 3	Level 4
Example of Service Levels	Mission Critical	Business Critical/ Effectiveness	Business Operational/ Efficiency	Office Productivity/ Administrative
Financial Loss	significant	significant	nominal	nominal
Recovery Cost	significant	nominal	significant	nominal
Criticality to Product Delivery	significant	significant	nominal	minimal
Customer Impact	significant	nominal	nominal	minimal

Based on the characteristics of the above service levels, systems must be classified in the minimum sufficient service level. However, this does not preclude a system from being promoted to a higher level of service if a client supports it or if one of the characteristics demands it. For instance, although a system may not have a significant impact on a customer, the exposure to financial loss may be so high that it must be handled at Level 1 service.

Each of the service levels listed above can be depicted as follows:

Level 1—Mission-Critical systems MUST be nonstop, and the loss of these applications will immediately affect the ability of the enterprise to deliver on its corporate mission. Virtually any cost is acceptable to maintain these applications against any likely risk.

Level 2—Business-Critical/Effectiveness business systems support the enterprise in the effective performance of the day-of-operations, but do not have a direct effect on operations (possibly because there are manual alternatives, etc.). These systems tend to be extremely time-sensitive and help the company avoid unnecessary crisis situations. The target availability for these applications is the same, nonstop. However, since the enterprise could function without these systems (maybe at considerably increased cost or effort), the effort to reach that target may be subordinated to maintaining mission-critical applications, or certain levels of risk may be acceptable due to extreme costs.

Level 3—Business Operational/Efficiency systems are used to run the business more efficiently. For short periods (e.g., less than a day), the loss of these applications will not prevent accomplishing the corporate mission package delivery. However, long-term loss of these systems will certainly impact the efficiency of the business, and cause large financial losses. Typically, these are planning and support operations and the activities they support are usually performed during normal business hours.

Level 4—Office Productivity/Administration systems provide the ability of employees to be creative, communicate, and productively work within the office environment. These systems do not have the compelling business importance to justify the costs and controls imposed by the higher service levels. However, this does not imply that some of the systems typically considered as part of this classification, such as e-mail and productivity applications, belong in this service level. If a system in a higher service level is highly dependent on such an application such as e-mail to deliver information, then the e-mail application components supporting this system must be classified in the same level of service as the system.

Guidelines will be specified at each level of service to determine the minimum acceptable metric that supports a given service level. It is the responsibility of the IT organization to ensure that these guidelines are met for systems in each level of service once a system is deployed into production.

11.3.2 Service Metrics

Each service offering should have some method of being measured. The old management proverb of, "if you can't measure it, you can't manage it," is very true.

In order to capture the metrics of the services that will be used to support/enable, a table, similar to Table 11–2 below can be very useful.

Table 11–2   Measuring Service Offerings

	Estimate	Unit of Measure	Additional Requirements	Metric—How will this be measured
Forecasted transaction volumes				
On-line response time				
Forecasted disk requirements				
Report printing				
Report delivery and performance				
System availability				
Tech support provided				
Maintenance of user IDs				
Backup & recovery requirements				
Disaster recovery				
Performance & tuning services				

Once the level of service for the system to be supported has been determined, a specific set of metrics can be established for the functional service to be offered. An example of the documentation of such a set of metrics is shown in Table 11–3.

Table 11–3 Service Metrics

Functional Service		Technical Operations Support		
Service Description		Provides second-level resolution support for all system platform, network, database, and other networked system devices.		
Service Level:				
Attributes/ Criteria	Mission Critical (1)	Business Critical (2)	Business Efficiency (3)	User Administered (4)
Support initiated	Proactive and immediate	Immediate <1 hour	< 4 hours	Within 2 business days
Customer Call	Response already in progress	Immediately documented	Immediately documented	Immediately documented
Support	On-site and dedicated	Emergency response teams	Field Service	Field Service
OS, NOS, and Middleware Code	Always available	Always available	Available when appropriate	Available when appropriate

11.4 When Have You Reached Success?

Early two-way communication between the user and the IT service provider is essential to ensure that success is continually pursued. Understanding the needs of the user from a business and technology standpoint will provide an awareness of needs in a more proactive mode. Going back to the first paragraph of this chapter, success is achieved only when the user says it has been achieved. So, the user or IT service consumer is the "Mom" in the analogy and no one should be happy until success has been declared.

We have discussed how to define success, how to ensure it is achieved, and how to measure it—now we address how to determine that you have achieved it. "Happiness" is very challenging to define, as it varies depending on individual perception and is susceptible to frequent change.

11.4.1 Service Satisfaction Survey

The traditional method of determining customer satisfaction or happiness is through surveys. This is an approach that should not be ignored, but should not be the only method utilized either, as it may become mechanical and result in little useful information.

Satisfaction surveys should be developed by a professional skilled in survey design and construction. Poorly executed satisfaction surveys can cause more damage than good. The survey should contain the following elements and provide for comments for each element as well as a quantitative ranking:

- Overall satisfaction with IT service
- Value added to your operation by IT
- Reliability of IT service
- Responsiveness of IT service
- List inhibitors to the use of IT service
- Ease of using IT service
- Frequency of recommending IT service to peers

Another approach or method to gauging customer satisfaction is a brief introspective quiz outlined in the book, *Building the New Enterprise*.[2]

- What's the size of your service request backlog? This can best be measured by volume of requests or in gross time outlooked to complete.
- Are customers resisting serving on your review boards and committees?
- Do customers control their share of your IT budget or does IT dictate priorities and project funding?
- Does the customer have a choice of service levels, and are there auditable metrics on the quality of service?

---

2. Harris Kern, Randy Johnson, Stuart Gulp, and Dennis Horan, *Building the New Enterprise*, SunSoft Press, 1998.

- Are customers going around IT departments by setting up local mini-IT functions?
- Are you having trouble getting support for your initiatives and budget requests?
- When you implement a new system, does the complaining die away in days, weeks, months, or never?
- How often do you have major system outages of multiple hours or even days in duration?

The surveys will provide documented evidence of success, as will reports of metric and SLA requirement accomplishment. Equally or perhaps more importantly is maintaining a positive relationship and frequent and open communications with key user personnel at all levels. The role of the account management function is invaluable in maintaining a "soft SLA" that will ensure that not only the documented service agreements are met, but that user expectations are satisfied on all levels.

11.4.2 Continuous Success

Achieving success should not be a one-time or periodic milestone to be checked off the proverbial to-do list, but a dynamic, ongoing effort.

In constructing ISD systems one must realize that the target is always moving, and adjustments must be made accordingly. Regular reviews of SLA, internal processes, staff skills, expertise, and leverageable technology will be required. But even more than these exercises, there must be attitudinal adjustments to keep service improvement continuous and users continuously happy.

Be proud of your successes. Take time out of the daily grind to celebrate them. Reward those that have been the primary contributors to this success and give them recognition in the presence of the user and their peers.

Lessons Learned—Key Messages

▶ ## 12.1 Overview

Much can be said for lessons learned. We live in a world that is completely obsessed with reduce, reuse, and recycle. So why limit this to only paper or plastic; why not include knowledge and processes as well? It is in this spirit that you should view this book. Not every word of every chapter may apply to your business circumstances; however, you should reduce your effort to develop processes from scratch and reuse and recycle proven and successful processes that exist wherever possible.

Essentially, this whole book conveys lessons learned with respect to development and implementation of an ISD model and associated strategy. Everything in this chapter is covered in detail throughout this book. This chapter is really meant to highlight the key messages. You will notice some redundancy below, but this is a result of the tightly integrated processes and services.

12.2 Processes

Strong, repeatable processes will allow you to define and maintain your portfolio of services and help you to organize yourself to successfully deliver these services predictably, efficiently, and cost-effectively.

- Services should be definable, stable, and measurable.
- Plan for success.
- Take a "customer approach."
- Establish a strong communication and feedback loop.
- Establish and maintain coalitions.
- Develop and maintain an accurate and complete services model and resource model.

12.3 People

Managing the human aspects of any project or initiative is the most challenging and the most rewarding undertaking. Everything we do centers around people: establishing coalitions, gaining buy-in, getting sign-off, productivity, staffing, etc. To summarize:

- Establish coalitions and gain buy-in early.
- Staff your team strategically.
- Test the market for resource availability.
- Establish a strong communication and feedback loop.

12.4 Communication

Enough cannot be said about *overcommunicating*. Almost every process related to a root cause analysis exercise ultimately points back to communication as a root cause. It is with this in mind that you should proactively address this problem by making communication part of your strategy upfront.

- Establish coalitions and gain buy-in early.
- Overcommunicate.
- Establish a strong communication and feedback loop.
- Establish and maintain coalitions.

12.5 Technology

Technology "refreshes" itself about every six months. Think about it: Just about the time you are putting in "new" technology and its associated services and processes, you are already behind. This is certainly not something new to think about; you have probably been chasing this for a few years. The real lesson here is not to get caught up in chasing technology. At the risk of being redundant, establishing strong, repeatable processes will allow you to define and maintain your portfolio of services, and help you to organize yourself to successfully deliver these services predictably, efficiently, and cost-effectively. Achieve this, and you will achieve the ultimate goal: customer satisfaction and loyalty!

Frequently Asked Questions (FAQ)

Q. *Why is it so important to spend so much time on developing a service strategy?*

A. With technology so widespread and readily available today, competitive advantage must be sought through other avenues. These days, a main competitive advantage comes through customer care and satisfaction. Whether it is PCs, appliances, cars, or computing operations services, customers all want to be "handled with care," to be satisfied. How many times have you been willing to pay more for a good or service because your level of satisfaction was so high? If the customer is not satisfied with the goods or services you provide, you can be sure they will either be looking elsewhere or escalating their concerns. It is for this reason that you must take a customer approach.

Q. *Which part of the organization would own this process?*

A. We developed a "new" organization within the IT organization called Integrated Service Delivery (ISD). This organization is cross-program and cross-department and should report in at a high enough level to be able to efficiently leverage and share resources and services.

Q. What makes a successful outsource partnership?

A. Outsourcing makes the most sense in an environment, business area, or set of services that is definable, stable, and measurable. If these factors are lacking, then your outsource partner will not be able to provide the timely delivery of quality, predictable services in a cost-effective manner. The key word here is *partnership*.

Q. Why are some outsourcing ventures unsuccessful?

A. There can be many reasons for an outsourcing venture to be unsuccessful. If you analyze the root cause of each, it is most likely poorly defined requirements that lack the appropriate metrics. Or, the environment is not stable and has ever-changing requirements. Both of these will drive level-of-service issues and could even affect cost.

Q. Communication throughout IT is worse than ever before. What can be done?

A. Establish service-level agreements and metrics upfront and maintain frequent and comprehensive communications on performance against the agreed targets. It is also extremely important to ensure that you have the appropriate processes, associated tools, and documentation necessary to report and track customer requirements and issues. A well-documented and easily executable escalation procedure is a good example of this.

Q. What are the minimum set of processes required to have a cost-effective enterprise?

A. The minimum set of processes are a function of the comprehensiveness of the services that are required to adequately support the business and the level of service to be provided. Problem Management, Change Management, and Production Acceptance (CMPA)[1] are among the top processes to consider.

---

1. Harris Kern and Randy Johnson, *Rightsizing the New Enterprise*, SunSoft Press, 1994.

Q. How can risk be minimized when moving to a different technology environment?

A. A technology shift is something that cannot happen from the bottom up, it must happen from the top down. Gaining early and complete buy-in from the highest level of management is, therefore, essential. To truly minimize the risk, it is essential that you first understand the set of customer requirements, or technical requirements, that you will be satisfying with the technology move. Once you understand how you will be applying the technology, you can organize, staff, and train appropriately. Stay focused on satisfying the customer!

Q. Outsourcing vendors are telling executive management that they can manage their infrastructure more efficiently. Is this the case?

A. Whether or not you should look at outsourcing vendors depends largely on the stability, definabilty, and measurability of the infrastructure. As detailed in Chapter 1, if you cannot define what you want, chances are an outsource vendor will have less success. Customer satisfaction should be the gauge by which you base your decisions. If you are dealing with a well-defined and stable infrastructure experiencing a predictable amount of change, and your internal IT shop is not delivering the expected level of service, then outsourcing vendors will definitely be appealing to management.

Q. I manage the IT infrastructure at my company and my CIO comes from a development background. How can I convince her of the urgency to focus on an ISD model?

A. It all points to customer satisfaction. Take a hard look at what your customers are saying today about the services being offered by your IT organization. If you do not have concrete data, send out a survey and solicit real customer feedback. You will find that this survey will most likely support your suspicions, as well as the conversations you overhear in the hallway, regarding unsatisfied customers. Present these fact-based results to management, along with a course of action, and they will agree that change is neccessary.

Q. *I have had little success benchmarking. What is the best way to approach it?*

A. Computer operations in a global distributed environment is, relatively speaking, a new paradigm. Challenges exist with being able to clearly define the technical environment along with its associated portfolio of services. As a result, few benchmarks exist to use as a guide for setting up a successful operation.

Classic benchmarking efforts oriented to manufacturing-type environments can often be quite extensive, exhaustive, and expensive. In the rapidly changing and evolving IT environment, time is of the essence and return on investment is challenging to calculate. Apply a focused approach to benchmarking while retaining the following primary key steps:

- Establish the reason to benchmark.
- Develop an understanding of the current environment's needs.
- Identify appropriate target companies.
- Develop a methodology of collecting information.
- Commit to a plan of utilizing the information collected.

Q. *Our IT shop is growing very quickly and the pressure to try and keep up with business requirements is enormous. We know that we need to do the things you talk about in the book, but there is never enough time for even the minimum and sufficient set of processes. How should we approach this?*

A. You are in this situation for a reason, and there is really little choice. Running in a continuously reactive mode is not the answer. Have you ever heard the saying, *"No time to do it right, but plenty of time to do it over!"* I can almost assure you that the time that you do not have is being spent on "redoing" work that is not being done "right" the first time.

You need to make the time and start somewhere, and if we were to prioritize for you, we would start with first understanding your customer's requirements and delivery expectations. From here you can begin a ground-up approach to developing a service model, then move right into organizing and resourcing. Again, there are no "magic formulas." Start slowly. It might take you six months to a year to develop a model, but you do need to start. You can also phase the implementation incrementally to achieve benefit along the way.

Job Descriptions

A.1   Account Manager

Education

A relevant BS degree. A masters degree is preferred. As an alternative to a masters, candidates with previous experience in IT may also qualify.

Experience

Generally, 10–15 years of satisfactory performance in a related area and approximately 10 years of job experience to date. Experience should include exposure to commercial, administrative, or industrial work environments.

Skills

➤ Approximately 10 years of job experience to date, including some involvement with service delivery in manufacturing and/or ISC.

➤ Has demonstrated success as the leader of a technical staff engaged in at least one area of service delivery. Demonstrates competence in staff leadership and project leadership tasks.

➤ Demonstrates an in-depth knowledge of the organization's policy framework (including application, infrastructure, compute, and telecom), management structures, and reporting procedures for the service delivery environment.

➤ Possesses up-to-date knowledge of hardware and software. Can describe all aspects of the operational and developmental environments within the organization.

Performance Expectations

➤ Takes responsibility for a team or teams of technical staff involved in one or more of the following tasks:

- efficiently providing the agreed service levels for daily/routine requests taken at any significant combination of batch or on-line facilities
- operating and maintaining significant computer and communications networks
- designing procedures for maintaining user security, recovering and restarting (from disaster), and controlling incidental/problem control
- developing, testing, installing, and maintaining operational or developmental environments
- providing user services, support, and guidance in an operational, departmental, or personal computing environment
- controlling changes affecting IT systems, services, or facilities
- conducting research and development work to increase and improve IT facilities and services

➤ Accurately forecasts future requirements for service delivery resources, including staff, equipment, services, funds, and time. Ensures that assigned resources are properly utilized and accounted for and that up-to-date information on the use of resources is maintained.

➤ Directs subordinate staff and fosters positive attitudes among staff on quality and safety to ensure that delivered service meets agreed service levels. Monitors and evaluates quality of performance and product from all work within scope of responsibility. Briefs staff on their individual and team performance.

➤ Selects and applies appropriate planning tools to accurately estimate and plan the work of teams or project groups within agreed policies. Produces work plans according to required standards. Works with colleagues to produce/recommend/develop long-term plans for operational and support areas.

➤ Matrix manages cross-functional suppliers: contracts, third-party consultants, etc., in delivering solutions.

➤ Monitors and reports on the progress of the resolution of high impact problems according to established standards. Handles those exceptions that have been referred from below relating to schedules, working methods, resources, staff matters, or technical difficulties. Passes decisions clearly outside scope upwards, including proposed solutions whenever appropriate.

➤ Conducts technical interviews and individual assessments for the recruitment and selection of IT staff. Manages the training and development of staff members so that the development of individuals benefits both the organization and the individual concerned.

➤ Maintains knowledge of hardware, software, organizational policies, and organizational management structures and uses this knowledge to advise on and justify their current use. Advises on and justifies proposed configuration specifications, strategic plans, and tactical plans, affecting service delivery.

➤ Writes and speaks fluently on all aspects of work. Communicates effectively with users/customers, colleagues 2–3 levels up/down and across a range of disciplines, and all levels of management. Directly negotiates with and functions as a liaison between clients, users, and suppliers.

➤ Develops and plans IT costs and accepts full accountability for all customers' IT, including annual planning processes for telecom, compute, infrastructure, new applications development and deployment, and applications support.

➤ Acts professionally at all times and encourages professional standards among subordinate staff.

Training and Development

> ➤ Obtains continuing training in those management skills needed to accept further responsibility for activities within service delivery. Particular emphasis should be placed on planning skills, risk management, safety-related issues, change control, financial management, and staff selection.

> ➤ Maintains up-to-date knowledge of all aspects of IT that impacts the operational and developmental environments, particularly those aspects assisting productivity and service quality.

> ➤ Obtains broad management and business training in those skill areas needed to function effectively in the environment of senior management.

> ➤ Successfully completes trial experiences that involve those skills of higher competency required at the next level of advancement.

▶ A.2 Oracle System Administrator (OSA)

Education

A relevant BS degree preferred. As an alternative, candidates with previous experience in IT may also qualify. The quality of the experience as demonstrated by achievement may compensate for lack of formal education.

Experience

Generally, one year of satisfactory performance in a related area and approximately one to two years of job experience to date. Experience should include exposure to commercial, administrative, or industrial work environments.

Skills

> ➤ Demonstrates knowledge in the use of computer systems and an aptitude for computer work.

> ➤ Demonstrates an authoritative and professional manner in telephone communication.

> ➤ Adheres to procedures, maintains records, and demonstrates commitment to solving user problems.

> ➤ Demonstrates a systematic, disciplined, and analytical approach to problem solving.

Performance Expectations

> ➤ Service request management (help desk)

- Accepts telephone calls from users who are requesting information or requesting services related to products, services, and facilities. Investigates complex situations to diagnose underlying causes and assists users in recovering or continuing operation.

- Maintains accurate, consistent, and up-to-date records of all calls regarding user requests; updates these records as problems are resolved and users notified.

- Given a user request that cannot be directly resolved: refers request to the appropriate colleagues or service suppliers with the necessary diagnostic information.

- Using personal judgment, applies guidelines to prioritize the resolution of user requests.

- Monitors the progress of those problems referred to other colleagues or service suppliers and keeps users informed of progress through to resolution. Applies escalation procedures for problems not achieving satisfactory progress.

- Provides users with information on IT system updates and known system errors.

- Produces bulletins to inform users of changes in system availability, new facilities, and common problems.

- Maintains an up-to-date database of common user requests, difficulties, and known solutions.

- Monitors records of user requests to measure service levels and identify common problems needing management attention.
- Provides level of service and metric reporting. Reviews the performance of the help desk against agreed upon service levels and its planned performance.
- Recommends changes to immediate management to improve service levels provided by the help desk.

➤ Establishes and maintains user profiles and accounts

- Creation of new and maintenance of old accounts for UNIX, NT, and application accounts. Setup of account security. Account deletion. Assign UNIX groupings. Setup of application responsibilities, user menus, default printer. Reset passwords at UNIX, NT, application levels. Follow established security plans and processes.

➤ Oracle application management

- Provides tier II support to end customers. Investigates and resolves application alert messages. Investigates and resolves application processing errors and warnings.
- Monitors for down concurrent mangers. Registers and configures printers within the application. Defines report sets. Defines data purges. Incorporates software customizations into application software.

➤ Job scheduling and execution

- Set up and maintain Oracle concurrent managers, application job schedules, and data interface processes.
- Track the job schedules and their executions times. Maintain a database of jobs and schedules to be executed. Optimize the scheduling of jobs to increase throughput/performance and balance workloads. Restart abnormal job ends.
- Publish overall job operational plan.

➤ Client "new application" installs and deinstalls

- Troubleshoots client-side problems associated with application access.
- Installs/deinstalls client-side application software. Sets up and configures client for network connection to application software. Provides/sets up keyboard mapping for application software.

- Tests client for connectivity to application server.
- Provides server backups
  - Tape management within the tape silo.
  - Off-site tape storage, tracking, and retrieval.
  - Notification of failed backups. Immediate corrective action upon failure.
  - Backup schedule creation and maintenance.
- Training support
  - Provide classroom training support. Arrange and set up classroom training facility. Coordinate the setup training database environments. Testing of all training workstations and PDS connections prior to class. Establish student login accounts.
  - Set up projection/training devices for instructor. Set up keyboard mappings as necessary.
  - Desk-side training support. New user startup training. Assist in workstation training. Provide and review training material validation.
- Demonstrates a calm, rational, and organized approach to tasks when under pressure.
- Takes full responsibility for the quality and timeliness of own work. Manages own time effectively to respond to user requests in a timely fashion and provides users with agreed levels of service.
- Applies the given standards, procedures, and tools to accomplish work assigned. Produces all required documentation for tasks completed, according to established standards. Guides less experienced staff in the use of these standards, procedures, and tools.
- Communicates in a clear, concise manner, both orally and in writing, with users/customers, colleagues, and immediate management regarding present issues, processes, solutions, and areas for improvement.

Training and Development

- Attends ongoing or advanced courses in commercial and industrial business practices and terminology, particularly terminology and practices directly relevant to the activities of the user community being supported.

➤ Attends ongoing training on those existing and newly introduced IT systems, products, services, hardware environments, and software environments supported by the help desk and used in service delivery processes.

➤ Develops knowledge of any related specialty areas (e.g., quality control, problem management, change management, and software development needs).

➤ Studies technique and IT concepts to increase knowledge and skills needed to support user (e.g., service level management and customer care).

➤ Increases professional knowledge and awareness by reading and participating in technical activities outside of immediate employment.

➤ Successfully completes trial experiences that involve those skills of higher competency required at the next level of advancement.

▶ A.3 System Administrator (SA)

Education

A relevant BS degree preferred. As an alternative, candidates with previous experience in IT may also qualify. The quality of the experience as demonstrated by achievement may compensate for lack of formal education.

Experience

Generally, one year of satisfactory performance in related area, and approximately one to two years of job experience to date. Experience should include exposure to commercial, administrative, or industrial work environments.

Skills

➢ Demonstrates an aptitude for systems work.

➢ Adheres to procedures, maintains records, and follows problems through to resolution.

➢ Demonstrates a systematic, disciplined, and analytical approach to problem solving.

➢ Demonstrates detailed knowledge of hardware and software architectures and their components, and can identify, explain, and address hardware and systems architectures, their components, and software development methods.

Performance Expectations

➢ Within a loosely supervised environment: Uses standard operating facilities, diagnostic tools, technical manuals, and system documentation to identify, diagnose, and solve basic system problems as directed.

➢ Can describe and document the operational environment, including:

- its architecture.
- external interfaces.
- communication aspects.

➢ Performs server performance tuning:

- Provide tier II and III support to the help desk for performance issues.
- Maintain historical information on server performance.
- Make adjustments to UNIX-level system parameters.
- Compile database statistics.
- Make adjustments to database to increase performance.
- Compile network performance metrics.
- Follow change control.
- Graphically illustrate resource usage by CPU, disk, memory, network, etc.

➢ Server monitoring and corrective action:

- Maximize server uptime.

- Ensure disk drive capacity within defined limits.
- Ensure network connectivity is alive and well.
- Ensure paging software is active.
- Ensure no "run away" processes.
- Ensure memory utilization is within defined limits.
- Ensure all databases are active after backup process.
- Detect problems or bottlenecks.
- Analyze performance compared to capacity.
- Provide tier II server level support.
- Troubleshoot database problems.
- Perform software event monitoring.
- Perform system and disk fault detection.

➤ Provide print services:
- Troubleshoot printer problems in the decentralized environment.
- Perform black box hookups.
- Perform software installation/configuration on new printers.
- Perform file server management of print queues.
- Provide spooling services including spooling software.
- Provide secured printing capability printing.
- Resolve printing problems.

➤ Provide application server support:
- Assist in software installs/upgrade.
- Assist in creation of scheduling jobs.
- Assist in directory setup.
- Assist in application tuning.
- Assist in job monitoring.
- Mount tapes on servers as required.

➤ Provide engineering support:
- Install and test new technologies.
- Provide support in the benchmark lab.
- Test interoperability of new hardware and software.
- Research new technologies and provide recommendations.

- Provide server security:
  - Design and oversee the implementation of printer security measures.
  - Design and oversee the implementation security measures on computing devices to protect individual hosts from unauthorized access.
  - Load external media to avoid introducing any viruses.
- Perform software distribution:
  - Create media for software distribution.
  - Test unloads of media before distribution.
  - Provide documentation of how to unload media.
  - Provide site assistance of unloading of software.
  - Document site requirements for software in which to execute.
  - Provide installation for application software.
  - Move site specific software into production when requested.
  - Follow change control process for production moves.
  - Assist development and DBA teams on production software installations.
- Demonstrates a calm, rational, and organized approach to tasks when under pressure.
- Manages own time effectively to respond to user requests in a timely fashion and provide users with agreed levels of service.
- Applies the given standards, procedures, and tools to accomplish work assigned. Produces all required documentation for tasks completed, according to established standards.
- Demonstrates excellent oral and written communication skills with users/customers, colleagues, and immediate management.

Training and Development

- Obtains instruction in the structure, business, and methods of the organization.
- Obtains instruction in any related areas of technical specialization.

- ➤ Obtains training in systems programming and support, the standard methods and tools of the organization, and service delivery processes.
- ➤ Attends courses covering relevant technical or specialist areas (e.g., hardware, systems software, technical architecture, tools, operating system functions, security, disaster recovery, communications/networking, performance engineering, and capacity management).
- ➤ Increases knowledge of IT and its uses within the organization.
- ➤ Increases professional knowledge and awareness by reading and participating in technical activities outside of immediate employment.
- ➤ Successfully completes trial experiences that involve those skills of higher competency required at the next level of advancement.

▶ A.4 Database Administrator (DBA)

Education

A relevant BS degree preferred. As an alternative, candidates with previous experience in IT may also qualify. The quality of the experience as demonstrated by achievement may compensate for lack of formal education.

Experience

Generally, two years of satisfactory work experience in related area and approximately four to six years of job experience to date. Experience should include substantial practical systems work with experience handling and analyzing data. Demonstrated skills in the development, use, and support of one or more database management systems.

Skills

➢ Adheres to procedures, maintains records, and follows problems through to resolution.

➢ Demonstrates a systematic, disciplined, and analytical approach to problem solving.

➢ Can describe data management concepts, modeling, and applications, including their benefits and potential use and value to the organization.

➢ Excellent communication skills and ability to interact with customers/users effectively.

Performance Expectations

➢ Can technically describe and apply data management concepts, modeling techniques and design principles. Can describe database architectures, software, facilities, and their applications currently used, in detail.

➢ Applies technical knowledge to carry out one or more of the following:

- Effectively uses selected DBMS, query languages, other DB tools and techniques as directed to complete work assigned.
- Works with users/customers and development project groups to interpret installation standards, produce database components, and meet project needs.
- Works with users/customers to define database requirements and other data management tools and facilities. Evaluates potential solutions, and demonstrates, installs, and commissions selected products to meet user/customer needs.
- Constructs, extends, or maintains tests, and corrects and documents software components of DBMS to achieve well-engineered products.

➢ Provides application database support:

- Perform analysis of application SQL code when requested.
- Representation of DBA in application team meetings.
- Inform application team of any system/database changes that might affect their application.

- Consult on application test procedures and test evaluation plan.
➤ Performs release scheduling and packaging:
  - Define operating and system level software to be incorporated in a release.
  - Prepare software for software distributions.
  - Prepare documentation to support software.
  - Work with application development team to prepare total release package.
  - Prepare listing of all software included in release.
  - Provide technical documentation as needed.
  - Provide instruction notes to install/set up specific application software.
  - Develop and document any software scripts needed.
  - Test software scripts before software distribution.
  - Ensure all packaging is complete before distribution.
➤ Performs database administration:
  - Sizing and creation of databases.
  - Table/index sizing and defragmentation.
  - Database capacity planning.
  - Define and implement backup and recovery process for database instance.
  - Database backup and restores.
  - Transform logical data model into physical data model.
  - Implement physical data model.
  - Document database as per standards.
  - Tune the database.
  - Provide tier II level support.
  - Troubleshoot database problems.
➤ Ensures database security:
  - Ensure Oracle account passwords are changed periodically.
  - Ensure passwords for DBA Oracle accounts are not hard-coded in files, SQL scripts, and documents.
  - Set up database security scheme.
  - Grant and revoke database access per security scheme.
  - Enable database audit trail tracking when necessary.

- Periodically review database access (users and tables access) to verify security scheme is being followed.
- Revoke database access when user is no longer associated with application.

➤ Demonstrates a calm, rational, and organized approach to tasks when under pressure.

➤ Manages own time effectively to respond to user requests in a timely fashion and provides users with agreed levels of service.

➤ Applies the given standards, procedures, and tools to accomplish work assigned. Produces all required documentation for tasks completed, according to established standards.

➤ Demonstrates excellent oral and written communication skills with users/customers, colleagues, and immediate management.

Training and Development

➤ Increases knowledge in the structure, business, and methods of the organization.

➤ Increases knowledge in any related areas of technical specialization.

➤ Increases technical or specialist knowledge in data management concepts, tools, applications, and other related areas (e.g., CASE tools, repositories, fourth generation environments, query languages, user interfaces, data communications, security).

➤ Increases knowledge of databases, particularly the roles that databases play in the areas of development, production support, service delivery, and the integration of databases within the local software environment.

➤ Obtains ongoing training and practice in oral, written, and project leadership skills.

➤ Increases knowledge of IT and its uses within the organization.

➤ Increases professional knowledge and awareness by reading and participating in technical activities outside of immediate employment.

➤ Successfully completes trial experiences that involve those skills of higher competency required at the next level of advancement.

A.5 Network Specialist (NS)

Education

A relevant BS degree preferred. As an alternative, candidates with previous experience in IT may also qualify. The quality of the experience as demonstrated by achievement may compensate for lack of formal education.

Experience

Generally, two years of satisfactory work experience in related area and approximately two to four years of job experience to date. Experience should include substantial practical systems work with leadership experience and experience in network and communications. Has successfully applied network/communications concepts, data modeling, and data management applications in a variety of situations.

Skills

> Can describe in detail network topologies and their use.
> Excellent interpersonal and communication skills and ability to interact with customers/users effectively.
> Can describe in detail all IT concepts and practices, including their interdependencies.

Performance Expectations

> Can describe and apply technical and application knowledge of data management concepts, modeling techniques, and design principles to complete project work. Can describe in detail database architectures, software, facilities, and applications and their value to the organization.

➤ Applies technical knowledge and skills to address complex and nonstandard situations to two or more of the following:

- Provides advice and guidance to users and upper managers on the use of network/communications facilities to enhance business solutions.
- Works with colleagues to develop communications strategies and standards for significant projects or major application areas.
- Provides specialty technical support to service delivery functions in the planning, modeling, demonstration, installation, and customization of IT products.
- Works with teams to assist users/customers in identifying requirements for network/communications hardware, software, services, and facilities.
- Advises users/customers on the feasibility, practicality, and cost-effectiveness of the options proposed.
- For complex network/communications systems: manages small teams of staff to complete all stages of the life cycle for hardware/software development (including investigation, analysis, specification, design, construction, testing, maintenance, upgrade, and migration) to achieve well-engineered products.
- Provides staff teams with expertise in the development, use, and operation of network/communication tools and facilities. Manages the work of small teams to deliver quality project work and services on time and within budget.

➤ Provides network management:

- Analysis of network impacts based on new adds and changes.
- Maintain a network topology drawing.
- Manage new installations/connects to network.
- Network capacity planning.
- Set up and maintain modem connections.
- Control the granting and revoking of modem access from outside.
- Provide naming services resolution.

- ➤ Utilizes specialized techniques, tools, methods, and standards as needed to address organizational and user/customer needs for quality, security, availability, integrity, and safety.

- ➤ Demonstrates a calm, rational, and organized approach to tasks when under pressure.

- ➤ Manages own time effectively to respond to user requests in a timely fashion and provide users with agreed levels of service.

- ➤ Applies the given standards, procedures, and tools to accomplish work assigned. Produces all required documentation for tasks completed, according to established standards.

- ➤ Demonstrates excellent oral and written communication skills with users/customers, colleagues, and immediate management.

Training and Development

- ➤ Maintains knowledge and skills in networks/communications through active participation in seminars, conferences, workshops, etc.

- ➤ Maintains up-to-date theoretical and practical specialty network/communications knowledge.

- ➤ Maintains detailed knowledge of a wide range of network/communication software, hardware, media, services, and facilities available and in development.

- ➤ Obtains ongoing training and practice in oral, written, and project leadership skills; attends management training.

- ➤ Increases knowledge of IT and its uses within the organization.

- ➤ Increases professional knowledge and awareness by reading and participating in technical activities outside of immediate employment.

- ➤ Successfully completes trial experiences that involve those skills of higher competency required at the next level of advancement.

A.6 Operational Manager (Ops Mgr)

Education

A relevant BS degree preferred. As an alternative, candidates with previous experience in IT may also qualify. The quality of the experience as demonstrated by achievement may compensate for lack of formal education.

Experience

Generally two years of satisfactory work experience in related area and approximately 10–14 years of job experience to date, which includes exposure to relevant commercial, administrative, or industrial work environments. Experience must have included a position of responsibility that provided insight into service delivery from both a user and provider viewpoint.

Skills

> Demonstrates a good understanding of the organization's policy framework, technical environment, management structures, and procedures for service delivery.
> Demonstrates ability in the responsible management of service delivery and excellent communication and negotiation skills.

Performance Expectations

> Manages teams of staff to deliver the quantity and quality of services delivered according to written level of service agreements between users and suppliers for a defined organizational unit.
> Defines the mapping of services to users to establish the structure of service level agreements for the organization, ensures that a catalogue of all available services is created and maintained.

- Determines service level requirements for each area subject to an agreement using specialist planners and experts where necessary.
- For each service level agreement: negotiates cost-effective service levels such as quantity (hours, times, throughput, consumable) and quality (availability, reliability, performance, capacity for growth, user support, contingency, security) and obtains signatures to the service level agreements.
- Monitors service levels achieved, ensures records are maintained and analyzed, initiates actions, and issues reports on achievement to users, providers, and management.
- Periodically reviews all service level agreements to ensure continued meeting of targets in a cost-effective manner and to balance overall user requirements with current and planned services.
- When service is provided by external suppliers: negotiates contracts to provide service levels required, establishes problem resolution procedures and defines the consequences of non-compliance.
- Customer Interface
  - Provide level of service management
  - Management of level of service agreements
  - Tracking of LOS
  - Execution of LOS
  - Reporting of LOS
  - Conduct service level reviews
  - Conduct customer satisfaction survey
  - Maintain a service improvement plan
  - Maintain a service publication
  - Provides cost management
  - Maintain chargeback model
  - Ensure new transfer agreements are in place
  - Renew yearly transfer agreements
  - Ensure revenue is received from customers
  - Cost reporting to customer and management
- Procure Hardware
  - Assist customer on procurement of hardware
  - Verify hardware compatibility with current environment
  - Procure necessary equipment for data center operations

➤ Manage Facilities

- Design and oversee the implementation of security measures on network devices to protect data center systems from unauthorized access
- Perform ongoing security audits to ensure that data center security is maintained at proper levels
- Monitor security-related information sources for timely warnings of possible security holes
- Respond to any suspected security-related problem
- Disaster recovery planning
- Computer room space planning
- Ensure adequate power, light, and air conditioning

➤ Manages own time effectively to respond to user requests in a timely fashion and provide users with agreed levels of service.

➤ Demonstrates excellent oral and written communication skills with users/customers, colleagues, and immediate management.

Training and Development

➤ Maintains knowledge of all relevant aspects of IS and expands areas of specialty knowledge (e.g., quality management, availability management, capacity planning, contingency planning, facilities management).

➤ Seeks knowledge of all software and hardware products and services that may affect future strategy or policies.

➤ Obtains management and financial training in order to establish a good understanding of the context within which investment recommendations are made.

➤ Increases knowledge of IT and its uses within the organization.

➤ Increases professional knowledge and awareness by reading and participating in technical activities outside of immediate employment.

➤ Successfully completes trial experiences that involve those skills of higher competency required at the next level of advancement.

▶ A.7 Customer Services Manager (CS Mgr)

Education

A relevant BS degree preferred. As an alternative, candidates with previous experience in IT may also qualify. The quality of the experience as demonstrated by achievement may compensate for lack of formal education.

Experience

Generally, two years of satisfactory work experience in related area and approximately 8–12 years of job experience to date, which includes exposure to relevant commercial, administrative, or industrial work environments. Experience must have included a position of responsibility that provided insight into service delivery from both a user and provider viewpoint.

Skills

➤ Demonstrates a good understanding of the organization's policy framework, technical environment, management structures, and procedures for service delivery.
➤ Demonstrates ability in the responsible management of service delivery and excellent communication and negotiation skills.

Performance Expectations

➤ Manages staff teams to deliver the quantity and quality of services delivered according to written level of service agreements between users and suppliers for a defined organizational unit.
➤ Defines the mapping of services to users to establish the structure of service level agreements for the organization; ensures that a catalogue of all available services is created and maintained.

- Determines service level requirements for each area subject to an agreement using specialist planners and experts where necessary.
- For each service level agreement: negotiates cost-effective service levels such as quantity (hours, times, throughput, consumable) and quality (availability, reliability, performance, capacity for growth, user support, contingency, security) and obtains signatures to the service level agreements.
- Monitors service levels achieved, ensures records are maintained and analyzed, initiates actions, and issues reports on achievement to users, providers, and management.
- Periodically reviews all service level agreements to ensure continued meeting of targets in a cost-effective manner and to balance overall user requirements with current and planned services.
- Manages help desk operations
  - Schedule 24 × 7 help desk coverage.
  - Ensure all service levels are met.
  - Ensure closure on all escalated problem calls.
  - Manage OSA desk-side operations.
  - Schedule OSA coverage.
  - Ensure all service levels are met.
- Manages own time effectively to respond to user requests in a timely fashion and provide users with agreed levels of service.
- Demonstrates excellent oral and written communication skills with users/customers, colleagues, and immediate management.

Training and Development

- Maintains knowledge of all relevant aspects of IS and expands areas of specialty knowledge (e.g., quality management, availability management, capacity planning, contingency planning, facilities management).
- Seeks knowledge of all software and hardware products and services that may affect future strategy or policies.
- Obtains management and financial training in order to establish a good understanding of the context within which investment recommendations are made.
- Increases knowledge of IT and its uses within the organization.

➤ Increases professional knowledge and awareness by reading and participating in technical activities outside of immediate employment.

➤ Successfully completes trial experiences that involve those skills of higher competency required at the next level of advancement.

Sample Service Level Agreement

REVISION DATE: 6 August, 1999			
Area of Responsibility		Signature	Date
Customer: *Mfg Plant Mgr*	Nicole Sano	_____	
Customer Functional Mgr:	Shannon Kullmann	_____	
IT Program Mgr:	Jonathan Matthews	_____	
IT ISD Mgr:	Paul Bardanis	_____	
IT Appl. Support:	Maria Tardugno	_____	

Section I: System Availability

Requirements	Description	Specifications
Customer Required Hours of Operation	The hours that the system needs to be operational. This includes on-line availability for end users and batch processing capabilities	End user on-line hours: 6 am to 11 pm, Monday through Sunday (Eastern Std. Time USA) Batch Processing hours: 2 am–6 am EST Monday through Sunday
System Server Availability	The hours that the system server will be available for processing	The system will be operational consistent with on-line and batch hours as noted above (reference Customer Required Hours of Operation). The server system availability target is 99%. The system will *not* be available for two hours daily (seven days a week) for scheduled backups and HW/SW system maintenance. Other scheduled outages if required will not be measured against server system availability percentage.
System Availability Locations	Sites that the system supports. Locations of workstations	Manufacturing Plant Buildings 100, 200, 300
Network Availability	This refers to the availability of the connectivity from servers to the customer workstation.	Network availability must be consistent with Customer Required Hours of Operation referenced above. Target network availability is 99.9%.

Section II: Problem Management

Services	Description	Specifications
Call Management Process	This is the process for the recording, diagnosis, tracking, and closure of Help Desk calls. This includes the flow of information, call severity definitions, and call resolution responsibilities. This covers from initial contact by the user to problem closure.	*Attachment A* describes the call management process flow and points of contact. See *Attachment B* for Call Severity Definitions. See *Attachment F* for Call Management Responsibilities
Help Desk Coverage Hours	The time the Help Desk will be available to accept calls	24 hours × 7 days a week.
Call Logging	This is the documenting of capture requests, symptoms, priority, contacts, and relevant information.	
Call Acknowledgment	The time for the Help Desk to contact the call originator, acknowledging that the call was received.	See *Attachment C* for Call Response Times table.
Production Support Team	Production Support provides the next level of support when the Help Desk cannot resolve the problem or request.	The following groups make up the Production Support Team: • IT ISD provides support for UNIX, DBA, and OSA issues. • IT Applications Support provides support for application-related support problems. • IT Functional Support Team provides assistance for functional and training issues and questions

(continued)

Appendix **B** I Sample Service Level Agreement

Services	Description	Specifications
Production Support Team Response and Callback	The Response and Callback time frame is the length of time for Production Support to respond and call back the customer. The call-back to the customer may be from the Help Desk after the Production Support Team responds. Note: The contacts for the Production Support Team must be provided to the Help Desk	The Production Support Team provides staffed coverage during the hours of 8 am to 5 pm Monday through Friday (Eastern Time USA, except per the division holiday schedule). For the nonstaffed hours, the response time for Priority 1 problems is within 2 hours. See *Attachment C* for Call Response Times table.
Status Calls	The Help Desk will provide updates on progress in resolving calls to identified personnel.	See *Attachment C* for Call Response Times table for the timing of status calls. See *Attachment D* for Status Call Contacts.
Resolution Target	The target time that it will take to resolve each call depending on priority.	See *Attachment B* for Call Response Times table.
Escalation Procedures	The escalation process is a management notification procedure that is invoked when a problem persists after the problem resolution Target time frame is exceeded.	See *Attachment E* for Escalation Contacts.

Section III: Support Services

Services	Description	Specifications
System Backups	The frequency and timing of SW and data backups	System SW and Data will be backed up daily between the hours of 11 pm and 2 am and stored offsite.
Capacity Planning	Identification and development of future capacity requirements to meet system business requirements and budgeting cycles.	Capacity planning requirements will be identified and reviewed at least twice annually as part of an overall resource optimization and budgetary planning process.

System Change Management	The process to manage and track system change requests to the servers and applications.	All systems change requests are to be submitted to the Help Desk. This functions as the control and tracking point for all changes. Change notification request periods are based on the type of change:
		• Major Projects:
		  Two (2) weeks prior to change date.
		• Nonemergency :
		  Five (5) days prior to change date.
		• Emergency Fix:
		  Submitted within 24 hours after the fix has been implemented

SLA Reporting	Reporting of key metrics provide server availability and incident tracking.	Reporting will be provided monthly
SLA Document Management	SLA change control tracking	See *Change Control* table at end of document

Attachment B: Problem Severity Definitions

Description:	Definitions:
All calls will be classified into the following severity levels: • Priority 1 • Priority 2 • Major • Ordinary • Requests Note 1: Priority 1 problems will be worked on a 24 × 7 basis until resolved. A customer contact must be assigned and be available on a 24 × 7 basis to assess alternative solutions and finalize problem resolution verification. Note 2: Priority 2 problems will be worked during regular local business hours by production support groups.	**Priority 1:** The ability to conduct business or service the customer has stopped. *Examples:* Server down, network down, database down, application down, concurrent mgrs. down. **Priority 2:** Service is seriously degraded but can continue its operation via a work-around or incremental resource for a short period of time before business stops. *Examples:* Extremely slow system performance, a piece of application functionality is down or has a "bug." **Major:** Service is lost by a single or small number of users, affecting significant business functionality. Problems or incidents where a work-around exists or can be developed with a small amount of incremental resources. **Ordinary:** Problem or incident where single users can operate some of the system activities normally, but a definite problem is identified. **Requests:** Any call from single users or site groups that are requesting a new service or some clarification (e.g., requesting a new user logon, a new printer setup, or the meaning of a system message).

Attachment C: Problem Resolution Control

Severity	Call Ack	Production Support Team Response On-Site/Pager Support	Target Resolution	Status Call
Priority 1	15 min	15 min/15 min	24 hours	Every 2 hrs
Priority 2	15 min	15 min/60 min	1–2 business days	Every 4 hrs
Major	15 min	15 min/Next business day	5–10 business days	Every 4 hrs
Ordinary	15 min	1 day/Next business day	Per agreed to plan	Upon closure
Service Request	15 min	1 day/Next business day	2–5 business days	Upon closure

These times are cumulative for incidents that are routed to the help desk.

Attachment D: Status Call Contacts

Problem Severity	People to Contact	
Critical 1	Call Originator: Customer Functional Manager: Shannon Kullmann IT Functional Support: Jonathan Matthews IT Applications Development Manager: Nicholas Tardugno	IT ISD Manager: Albie DiPasquale IT ISD Help Desk Manager: Benjamin Sano
Critical 2	Call Originator: Customer Functional Manager: Shannon Kullmann IT Functional Support: Jonathan Matthews IT Applications Development Manager: Nicholas Tardugno	IT ISD Manager: Albie DiPasquale IT ISD Help Desk Manager: Benjamin Sano
Major	Call Originator: IT Applications Development Manager: Nicholas Tardugno	IT ISD Help Desk Manager: Benjamin Sano
Ordinary	Call Originator: IT ISD Help Desk Manager: Benjamin Sano	

Appendix **B** I Sample Service Level Agreement

Attachment E: Escalation Contacts

The following people are contacted when the Problem Resolution Targets are exceeded:

Critical Problems:

Problem Severity	People to Contact
Customer Management	Paul Bardanis
IT Senior Management	Santina Kullmann
Customer	Nicole Sano
IT Functional Support	Jonathan Matthews
IT Applications Dev. Mgr.	Nicholas Tardugno
IT ISD Manager	Albie DiPasquale
IT ISD Help Desk Mgr.	Benjamin Sano

Major Problems:

Problem Severity	People to Contact
IT Functional Support	Jonathan Matthews
IT Applications Dev. Mgr.	Nicholas Tardugno
IT ISD Manager	Albie DiPasquale
IT ISD Help Desk Mgr.	Benjamin Sano

Document Revisions Record:		
Change Description	Requester	Date

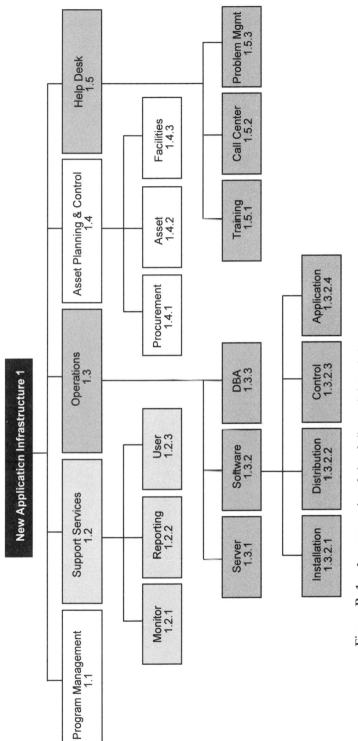

Figure B-1 An example of the full-work breakdown structure for an ISD organization.

Program Management 1.1

LOS Management 1.1.2
Management of level of service agreements
Tracking of LOS
Execution of LOS
Reporting of LOS
Conduct service level reviews
Conduct customer satisfaction survey
Maintain a service improvement plan
Maintain a service publication

Cost Management 1.1.1
Maintain charge back model
Ensure new transfer agreements in place
Renew yearly transfer agreements
Ensure revenue received from customers
Cost reporting to customer and management

Figure B–2   Breakdown of program management responsibilities.

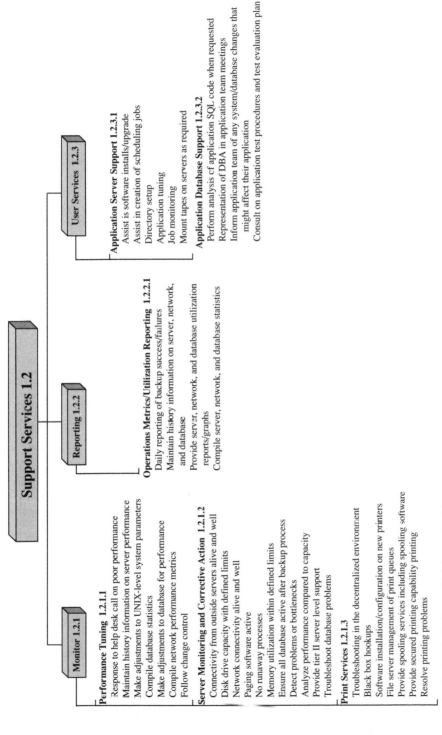

Support Services 1.2

Monitor 1.2.1

Reporting 1.2.2

User Services 1.2.3

Performance Tuning 1.2.1.1
Response to help desk call on poor performance
Maintain history information on server performance
Make adjustments to UNIX-level system parameters
Compile database statistics
Make adjustments to database for performance
Compile network performance metrics
Follow change control

Server Monitoring and Corrective Action 1.2.1.2
Connectivity from outside servers alive and well
Disk drive capacity with defined limits
Network connectivity alive and well
Paging software active
No runaway processes
Memory utilization within defined limits
Ensure all database active after backup process
Detect problems or bottlenecks
Analyze performance compared to capacity
Provide tier II server level support
Troubleshoot database problems

Print Services 1.2.1.3
Troubleshooting in the decentralized environment
Black box hookups
Software installation/configuration on new printers
File server management of print queues
Provide spooling services including spooling software
Provide secured printing capability printing
Resolve printing problems

Ongoing DB Monitoring and Maintenance 1.2.1.4
Database activity
Concurrent manager activity
ORASRV process alive and well
Listener server alive and well
Monitor for down databases
Monitor for down concurrent managers

Operations Metrics/Utilization Reporting 1.2.2.1
Daily reporting of backup success/failures
Maintain history information on server, network, and database
Provide server, network, and database utilization reports/graphs
Compile server, network, and database statistics

Application Server Support 1.2.3.1
Assist is software installs/upgrade
Assist in creation of scheduling jobs
Directory setup
Application tuning
Job monitoring
Mount tapes on servers as required

Application Database Support 1.2.3.2
Perform analysis of application SQL code when requested
Representation of DBA in application team meetings
Inform application team of any system/database changes that might affect their application
Consult on application test procedures and test evaluation plan

Figure B–3 Breakdown of support services responsibilities.

187

Appendix **B** | Sample Service Level Agreement

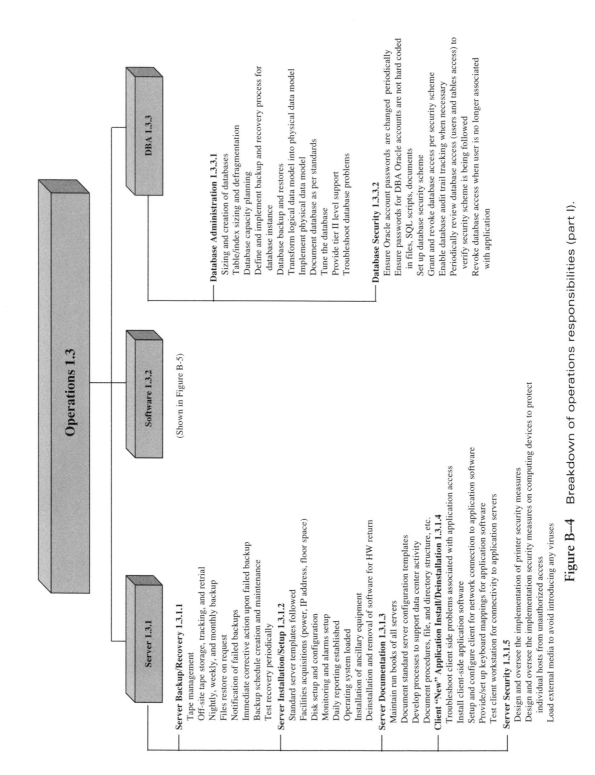

Operations 1.3

Server 1.3.1

Server Backup/Recovery 1.3.1.1
 Tape management
 Off-site tape storage, tracking, and retrial
 Nightly, weekly, and monthly backup
 Files restore on request
 Notification of failed backups
 Immediate corrective action upon failed backup
 Backup schedule creation and maintenance
 Test recovery periodically

Server Installation/Setup 1.3.1.2
 Standard server templates followed
 Facilities acquisitions (power, IP address, floor space)
 Disk setup and configuration
 Monitoring and alarms setup
 Daily reporting established
 Operating system loaded
 Installation of ancillary equipment
 Deinstallation and removal of software for HW return

Server Documentation 1.3.1.3
 Maintain run books of all servers
 Document standard server configuration templates
 Develop processes to support data center activity
 Document procedures, file, and directory structure, etc.

Client "New" Application Install/Deinstallation 1.3.1.4
 Troubleshoot client side problems associated with application access
 Install client-side application software
 Setup and configure client for network connection to application software
 Provide/set up keyboard mappings for application software
 Test client workstation for connectivity to application servers

Server Security 1.3.1.5
 Design and oversee the implementation of printer security measures
 Design and oversee the implementation security measures on computing devices to protect
  individual hosts from unauthorized access
 Load external media to avoid introducing any viruses

Software 1.3.2

(Shown in Figure B-5)

DBA 1.3.3

Database Administration 1.3.3.1
 Sizing and creation of databases
 Table/index sizing and defragmentation
 Database capacity planning
 Define and implement backup and recovery process for
  database instance
 Database backup and restores
 Transform logical data model into physical data model
 Implement physical data model
 Document database as per standards
 Tune the database
 Provide tier II level support
 Troubleshoot database problems

Database Security 1.3.3.2
 Ensure Oracle account passwords are changed periodically
 Ensure passwords for DBA Oracle accounts are not hard coded
  in files, SQL scripts, documents
 Set up database security scheme
 Grant and revoke database access per security scheme
 Enable database audit trail tracking when necessary
 Periodically review database access (users and tables access) to
  verify security scheme is being followed
 Revoke database access when user is no longer associated
  with application

Figure B-4 Breakdown of operations responsibilities (part I).

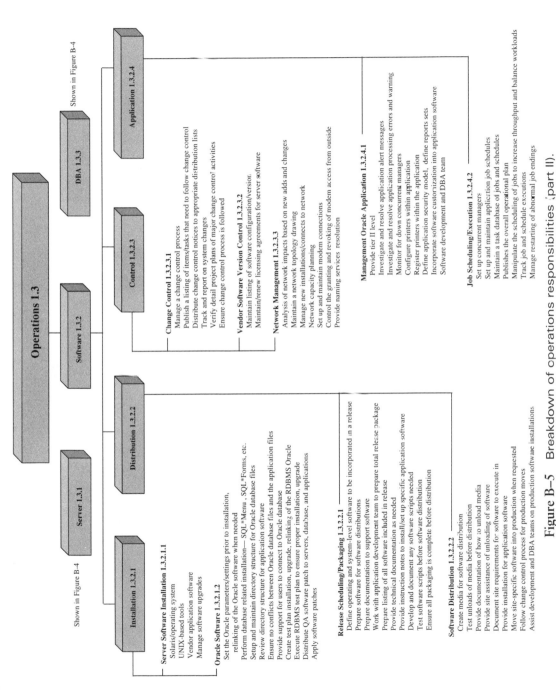

Figure B–5 Breakdown of operations responsibilities (part II).

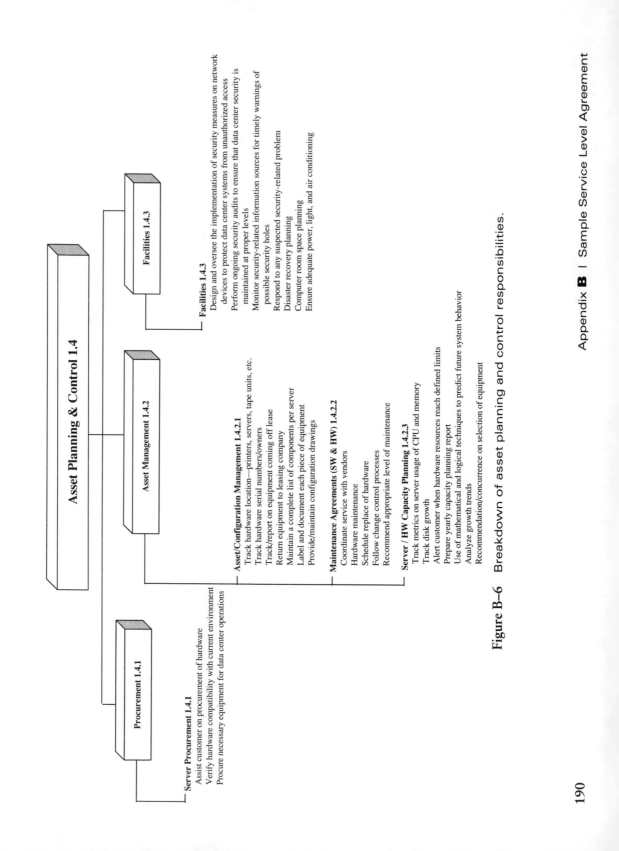

Asset Planning & Control 1.4

Procurement 1.4.1

Asset Management 1.4.2

Facilities 1.4.3

Server Procurement 1.4.1
Assist customer on procurement of hardware
Verify hardware compatibility with current environment
Procure necessary equipment for data center operations

Asset/Configuration Management 1.4.2.1
Track hardware location—printers, servers, tape units, etc.
Track hardware serial numbers/owners
Track/report on equipment coming off lease
Return equipment to leasing company
Maintain a complete list of components per server
Label and document each piece of equipment
Provide/maintain configuration drawings

Maintenance Agreements (SW & HW) 1.4.2.2
Coordinate service with vendors
Hardware maintenance
Schedule replace of hardware
Follow change control processes
Recommend appropriate level of maintenance

Server / HW Capacity Planning 1.4.2.3
Track metrics on server usage of CPU and memory
Track disk growth
Alert customer when hardware resources reach defined limits
Prepare yearly capacity planning report
Use of mathematical and logical techniques to predict future system behavior
Analyze growth trends
Recommendation/concurrence on selection of equipment

Facilities 1.4.3
Design and oversee the implementation of security measures on network
  devices to protect data center systems from unauthorized access
Perform ongoing security audits to ensure that data center security is
  maintained at proper levels
Monitor security-related information sources for timely warnings of
  possible security holes
Respond to any suspected security-related problem
Disaster recovery planning
Computer room space planning
Ensure adequate power, light, and air conditioning

Figure B–6 Breakdown of asset planning and control responsibilities.

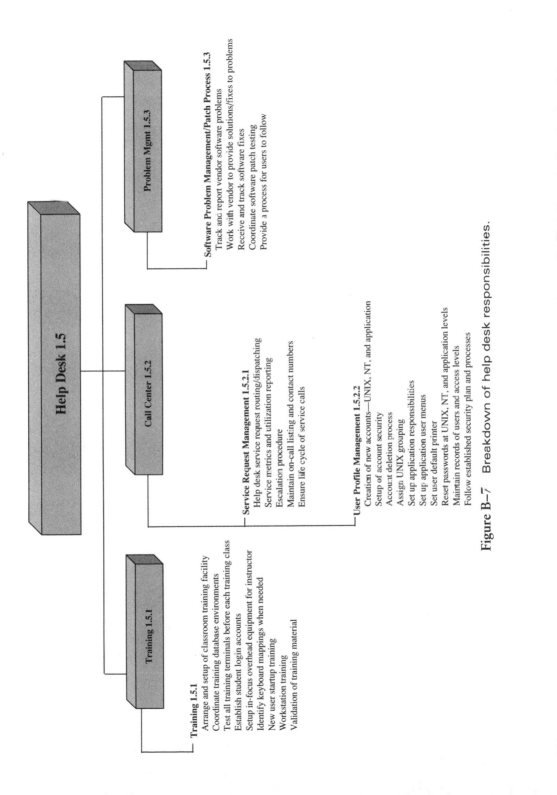

Training 1.5.1
Arrange and setup of classroom training facility
Coordinate training database environments
Test all training terminals before each training class
Establish student login accounts
Setup in-focus overhead equipment for instructor
Identify keyboard mappings when needed
New user startup training
Workstation training
Validation of training material

Service Request Management 1.5.2.1
Help desk service request routing/dispatching
Service metrics and utilization reporting
Escalation procedure
Maintain on-call listing and contact numbers
Ensure life cycle of service calls

User Profile Management 1.5.2.2
Creation of new accounts—UNIX, NT, and application
Setup of account security
Account deletion process
Assign UNIX grouping
Set up application responsibilities
Set up application user menus
Set user default printer
Reset passwords at UNIX, NT, and application levels
Maintain records of users and access levels
Follow established security plan and processes

Software Problem Management/Patch Process 1.5.3
Track and report vendor software problems
Work with vendor to provide solutions/fixes to problems
Receive and track software fixes
Coordinate software patch testing
Provide a process for users to follow

Figure B-7 Breakdown of help desk responsibilities.

Appendix **B** I Sample Service Level Agreement

Index

Team definitions, *(cont.)*

    extended support team, 15

    steering committee/decision team, 15

    support team, 15

Team member and vendor contact lists, 90–92

Technology, 147

Total effort hours, in cost model, 115

Traditional business framework, services in, 30–32

Training hours, in cost model, 115

V

Vacation hours, in cost model, 115

Value, 56

Variability, and insourcing vs. outsourcing decision, 5

Vendor contact lists, 90–92

Vendor resources, utilizing, 123

W

Workable hours calculation, in cost model, 115

Work breakdown structure, 25, 64–65

Work group, empowering, 17

Work package grouping example list, 66–68

Work packages, 64–65

Work process, defining, 19

X

Xerox Corporation, 69, 75, 100, 117